▲▲▲ THE MOUND BUILDERS

THE MOUND

Robert Silverberg

BUILDERS

Ohio University Press

Athens

The title-page picture is a painting on muslin by John J. Egan, 1850, now in the collection of the City Art Museum of Saint Louis. It was originally one panel in a painted panorama used as part of a popular traveling road show billed as "MONUMENTAL GRANDEUR OF THE MISSISSIPPI VALLEY, with scientific lectures on AMERICAN AERCHIOLOGY . . . THIS GORGEOUS PANORAMA with all the ABORIGINAL MONUMENTS of a large extent of country once roamed by the RED MAN..." The show was organized by Dr. Montroville Wilson Dickeson, an early excavator of the mounds of the Mississippi Valley.

The work is an abridged edition of
Mound Builders of Ancient America: The Archaeology of a Myth
by Robert Silverberg, published in 1968
by New York Graphic Society Ltd.

MAPS BY JEAN IVERS

Library of Congress Cataloging-in-Publication Data

Silverberg, Robert.
  The mound builders.

Reprint. Previously published: Greenwich, Conn.: New York Graphic Society, 1970.
  Abridged ed. of: Mound builders of ancient America.
  Bibliography: P.
  Includes index.
  1. Mound-builders—Juvenile literature. 2. Mounds—United States—Juvenile literature. 3. Adena culture—Juvenile literature. 4. Hopewell culture—Juvenile literature. 5. Mississippian culture—Juvenile literature. 6. Indians of North America—Antiquities—Juvenile literature. I. Silverberg, Robert. Mound builders of ancient America. II. Title.

[E73.S572 1986]   973.1   85-25953

ISBN 0-8214-0839-9

Ohio University Press books are printed on acid-free paper ∞

CONTENTS

▲▲▲

LIST OF ILLUSTRATIONS   6

1 THE DISCOVERY OF THE MOUNDS   9

2 THE MAKING OF THE MYTH   29

3 THE TRIUMPH OF THE MYTH   50

4 THE GREAT DEBATE   74

5 DEFLATING THE MYTH   125

6 THE HONORED DEAD:
   ADENA AND HOPEWELL   168

7 THE TEMPLE MOUND PEOPLE   233

   BIBLIOGRAPHY   268

   INDEX   270

   MAPS

      The de Soto explorations   20
      Adena sites   185
      Hopewell sites   203
      Temple Mound sites   236

5

LIST OF ILLUSTRATIONS

▲▲▲

Frontispiece—*Dr. Dickeson excavating a mound, from the Panorama of the Monumental Grandeur of the Mississippi Valley.* Painting on muslin by John J. Egan, 1850. Courtesy of the City Art Museum of Saint Louis.

1 Map of the de Soto explorations.

2 A Florida mound burial. Engraving by De Bry from a painting by Jacques Le Moyne, sixteenth century.

3 The great mound at Marietta. Engraving from *Ancient Monuments of the Mississippi Valley,* by E. G. Squier and E. H. Davis, 1848, from an early painting.

4 Diagram of the Newark works. Squier and Davis, 1848.

5 The Great Mound at Grave Creek. Engraving from *Ancient Monuments of the Mississippi Valley,* by E. G. Squier and E. H. Davis, 1848.

6 Diagram of the Fort Hill works. Squier and Davis, 1848.

7 Diagram of Wisconsin effigy mounds. Squier and Davis, 1848.

8 The Cincinnati tablet. Engraving from *Ancient Monuments of the Mississippi Valley,* by E. G. Squier and E. H. Davis, 1848.

9 De-Coo-Dah. Engraving from *Traditions of De-Coo-Dah,* by William Pidgeon, 1858.

10 An Ancient American battle-mound. Engraving from *Traditions of De-Coo-Dah,* by William Pidgeon, 1858.

11 Wisconsin elephant mound. Engraving from the *Second Annual Report of the Bureau of Ethnology.*

12 Manatee pipe, after Squier and Davis. Engraving from the *Second Annual Report of the Bureau of Ethnology.*

13 Manatee. Engraving from the *Second Annual Report of the Bureau of Ethnology.*

14 Raven pipe from Mound City.

15 Toucan, after Squier and Davis. Engraving from the *Second Annual Report of the Bureau of Ethnology.*

16 Davenport elephant pipe. Engraving from *A Vindication of*

6

the Authenticity of the Elephant Pipes and Inscribed Tablets, by Charles E. Putnam, 1885.

17 Copper ear plugs, Lauderdale County, Alabama.

18 Copper plate engraving from Etowah Mound, Georgia. From *Report on the Mound Explorations of the Bureau of Ethnology, Twelfth Annual Report*.

19 Shell disc with incised figure of mythical man-animal, Hale County, Alabama.

20 A Chronological Chart of the Prehistory of Eastern North America.

21 The Adena pipe.

22 Map of Adena sites.

23 The Berlin tablet.

24 The Great Serpent Mound. Aerial photograph.

25 The Serpent. Diagram, Squier and Davis, 1848.

26 Map of Hopewell sites.

27 Mound City group.

28 Diagram of the Mound City works. Squier and Davis, 1848.

29 Hopewell skull with copper nose from Seip Mound.

30 Pottery head from Seip Mound, Hopewell culture.

31 Gooseneck effigy pipe from Hopewell Mound Group.

32 Frog effigy pipe, Hopewell culture.

33 Owl effigy pipe, Hopewell culture.

34 Alligator effigy pipe from Esch Mound. Hopewell culture.

35 Bannerstone, Hopewell culture.

36 Copper fish, Hopewell culture.

37 Obsidian ceremonial blade from Hopewell Mound Group.

38 Bird claw in Mica, Hopewell culture.

39 A Hopewell burial showing necklaces.

40 Diagram of Fort Ancient. Squier and Davis. 1848.

41 Map of Temple Mound sites.

42 Effigy jar from Fortune Mound, Arkansas.

43 Effigy vessel from Pecan Point, Arkansas.

44 Kneeling man effigy from Temple Mound, Tennessee.

45 Effigy figure from Spiro Mound, Oklahoma.

46 Wooden antler mask from Spiro Mound, Oklahoma.

47 Shell gorget from Spiro Mound, Oklahoma.

48 Incised conch shell from Spiro Mound, Oklahoma.

49 Incised conch shell from Temple Mound, Oklahoma.

50 Temple Mound burials, Wycliffe, Kentucky.

51 Cahokia Mound, Illinois.

52 Effigy vessel from the Tennessee Valley.

53 Outer wall of the South Fort, Fort Ancient.

1

THE DISCOVERY
OF THE MOUNDS

▲▲▲

Monuments of past civilizations lie scattered in many parts of the world. Egypt has her pyramids, England her Stonehenge, Greece her Acropolis. Out of the jungles of Cambodia rise the towers of Angkor. The isle of Crete offers the sprawling palace of King Minos at Knossos. The stone cities of the Mayas adorn Mexico's Yucatán.

But in the continental United States we have few spectacular relics of prehistory. The only ancient settlements of the American Indian that have survived are in New Mexico and Arizona: the cliff dwellings of Mesa Verde, the giant "apartment houses" of Chaco Canyon, the many other sites of the people we call the Pueblo Indians. Outside the Southwest, though, the builders of ancient America worked in wood and earth, and little of their work has endured. For signs of our past we must look, not to vast monuments of imperishable stone, but to subtler things: the arrowhead in the forest soil, the image carved on the face of a cliff, the bit of broken pottery.

Our forefathers greatly regretted this lack when they came here in the seventeenth and eighteenth centuries. They

did not like to feel that they were coming into an empty
land peopled only by naked wandering savages. They
searched hopefully for traces of some grand and romantic
past. In Mexico and in South and Central America, European invaders had found great kingdoms and awesome
cities, but the land to the north seemed a continent only of
woods and plains, inhabited by simple huntsmen and equally
simple farmers. It offered no imagination-stirring symbols
of vanished greatness. In all this mighty continent, was there
nothing to compare with the antiquities of the Old World?

Men in search of a myth will usually find one, if they
work at it. In the fledgling Thirteen Colonies the mythmakers had little raw material with which to work; but as
the colonists gradually spread westward and southward,
they found strange earthen mounds, beyond the Alleghenies
and in the valley of the Mississippi, which could serve as
the inspiration for romantic tales of lost civilizations.

The mounds lacked beauty and elegance, perhaps. They
were mere heaps of earth. Some were colossal, like the
Cahokia Mound in Illinois, 100 feet high and covering 16
acres; others were mere blisters rising from the earth. Some
stood in solitary grandeur above broad plains, while others
sprouted in thick colonies. All were overgrown with trees
and shrubbery, so that their outlines could barely be distinguished, although, once cleared, the mounds revealed
their artificial nature by their regularity and symmetry of
shape. Within many of them were human bones, weapons,
tools, jewelry.

There were so many of these earthen heaps—ten thousand in the valley of the Ohio River alone—that they
seemed surely to be the work of an energetic and ambitious
race. As the settlers fanned outward during the eighteenth

and early nineteenth centuries, they found scarcely an area that did not show traces of mound-building activity. The Atlantic coast, from North Carolina up through New England, had no mounds, but beyond the Alleghenies they were everywhere.

In the North, the mound zone began in western New York, and extended along the southern shore of Lake Erie into what now are Michigan and Wisconsin, and on to Iowa and Nebraska. In the South, mounds lined the Gulf of Mexico from Florida to eastern Texas, and were found up through the Carolinas and across to Oklahoma. The greatest concentration of mounds lay in the heart of the continent: Ohio, Illinois, Indiana, Missouri. There were lesser mound areas in Kentucky and western Tennessee. Nearly every major waterway of the Midwest was bordered by clusters of mounds.

To some of the settlers, the mounds were nuisances to be plowed flat as quickly as possible. To others, they were places of handy refuge in time of flood. But to the antiquarian, the mounds were the work of a vanished race which with incredible persistence had erected them in the course of hundreds of thousands of years and then had disappeared from the face of North America.

Why a vanished race?

Because the Indians of the mound area, as the settlers found them, were semi-nomadic savages, few in number and limited in ambition. They seemed obviously incapable of the sustained effort needed to quarry tons of earth and shape it into a symmetrical mound. Nor did these Indians have any traditions of their own about the construction of the mounds; when questioned, they shrugged, or spoke vaguely about ancient tribes.

By the early nineteenth century, hundreds if not thousands of mounds had been examined, measured, and partly excavated by the settlers whose imaginations were stirred by them. These pioneering mound studies revealed the extreme variety in the forms of the earthworks. Along the Great Lakes, the mounds tended to be low, no more than three or four feet high, and took the forms of gigantic birds, reptiles, beasts, and men. These huge image-mounds seemed quite clearly to be of sacred nature—idols, perhaps. Such effigies were common in Wisconsin, Michigan, and Iowa, more rarely seen in Ohio and Missouri, and scarcely found anywhere else.

To the south, in the valley of the Ohio River, the customary shape of the mounds was conical and their height might be anything from a few yards to 80 or 90 feet. Such mounds seemed at first glance to have been lookout posts or signal stations, but excavation showed that they always contained burials. Aside from the conical burial mounds, isolated mounds in the form of immense, flat-topped pyramids were sometimes found in the Midwest. Some were terraced, or had graded roadways leading to their summits. To their discoverers it appeared probable that the flat-topped mounds had once been platforms for temples long ago destroyed by the elements.

In the lower Mississippi area, conical mounds were scarce, and flat-topped pyramids were the rule. These imposing structures reminded their discoverers of the *teocallis,* the stone pyramids of Mexico; and their presence in the states bordering the Gulf of Mexico clearly indicated some link between the Aztec culture and that of the builders of the mounds.

In addition to the effigy mounds, the burial mounds, and

the temple mounds, two types of embankment were observed, mainly in the central Ohio-Indiana-Illinois-Missouri zone. On hilltops overlooking valleys, huge "forts" had been erected, with formidable walls of earth sometimes reinforced by stone. These obviously defensive works covered many acres. In lowland sites were striking geometric enclosures—octagons, squares, circles, ellipses—of a clearly nonmilitary nature. The lines of embankment were 5 to 30 feet high, and the enclosures had areas of as much as 200 acres. Running out from the enclosures were often parallel walls many miles long, forming great avenues.

The size of these structures astonished the early settlers. One great mound near Miamisburg, Ohio, 68 feet high and 852 feet in circumference at the base, was found to contain 311,353 cubic feet of soil; another, in Ross County, Ohio, was shown to consist of 20,000 wagonloads of earth. Ross County alone proved to have 500 mounds and 100 enclosures.

Theories about the mounds and their builders multiplied swiftly. One idea was based on the presence of effigy mounds in the North, conical mounds and geometrical enclosures in the Midwest, and Mexican-style flat-topped pyramids in the South. Did this mean the builders had migrated southward, building ever greater mounds as they went, and at last had left Florida and Georgia and Louisiana to become the founders of the rich Mexican civilization? To this notion was offered its opposite: that out of Mexico had come colonists who moved northward across the continent, at first building earthen mounds in the style of the *teocallis,* then gradually transforming or forgetting their ancestral culture and producing the conical mounds of Ohio, and finally petering out as builders of effigy mounds near the Canadian border. But no one could be sure of any of this.

The discovery of the mounds was profoundly satisfying. These artificial hills soon were cloaked in mystery and myth. They provided a link between the New World and the Old, for scholars hurried to their books to find evidence of mound building in ancient times, and they were not disappointed.

From Herodotus, writing about 450 B.C., came details of the burial of a Scythian king on the Russian plains: the mourners place the dead monarch and his treasures in a tomb, and then "they set to work and raise a vast mound above the grave, all of them vying with each other, and seeking to make it as tall as possible."

The Old Testament told how Canaanite tribes worshiped their deity in "high places"—and what were these "high places" if not temple mounds? Homer's *Iliad* related how Achilles heaped a great mound over the remains of his friend Patroclus, and how Hector, Patroclus' slayer, eventually was buried in such a mound as well. Alexander the Great, it was said, had spent a fortune to build a burial mound for his friend Hephaestion. The Roman Emperor Julian, who died in Asia in the year A.D. 363 while warring against the Persians, was buried beneath a "huge tumulus," or mound. Danish annals told of the mound burial of Denmark's first king in the middle of the tenth century. In Britain, antiquaries had long amused themselves by opening ancient mounds, which they called "barrows."

The discovery of the North American mounds connected the New World to Herodotus and Homer, to Rome and the Vikings, to England's barrows, to all the mounds of Europe and Asia that had been known for so long. It let loose a flood of speculation about the origin and fate of their builders. Learned men came forth to suggest that our land had been visited long ago by Hebrews, Greeks, Persians, Romans, Vikings, Hindus, Phoenicians—anyone, in short, who had ever built a mound in the Old World. If the Israelites had built mounds in Canaan, why not in Ohio? And what had become of the builders of the mounds? Why, obviously, they had been exterminated by the treacherous, ignorant, murderous red-skinned savages who even now were causing so much trouble for the Christian settlers of the New World.

In this way a myth was born that dominated the American imagination throughout the nineteenth century. The builders of the mounds were transformed into the Mound Builders, a diligent and gifted lost race. No one knew where the Mound Builders had come from or where they had gone, but the scope for theorizing was boundless. The myth took root, flourished and grew, even spawned a new religion; then the scientists took over from the mythmakers and hacked away the luxuriant growth of fantasies. The most vigorous demythologizer was the one-armed Major J. W. Powell, conqueror of the Colorado River and later founder of the Smithsonian Institution's Bureau of American Ethnology. When the Bureau put the myth of the Mound Builders to rest in the 1880's, it was with a certain regret. Powell himself sounded rather wistful in the 1890–91 *Annual Report of the Bureau of Ethnology:*

"It is difficult to exaggerate . . . the force with which the hypothetic 'lost races' had taken possession of the imaginations of men. For more than a century the ghosts of a vanished nation have ambuscaded in the vast solitudes of the continent, and the forest-covered mounds have been usually regarded as the mysterious sepulchres of its kings and nobles. It was an alluring conjecture that a powerful people, superior to the Indians, once occupied the valley of the Ohio and the Appalachian ranges, their empire stretching from Hudson bay to the Gulf, with its flanks on the western prairies and the eastern ocean; a people with a confederated government, a chief ruler, a great central capital, a highly developed religion . . . all swept away before an invasion of copper-hued Huns from some unknown region of the earth, prior to the landing of Columbus. . . ."

2

If more attention had been paid to the experiences of the first Europeans to visit the American mounds, the whole Mound Builder myth of a lost race might never have gained headway. In 1539, Hernando de Soto and an expedition of gold-seeking Spaniards landed in Florida and made their way through much of the Southeast, exploring a thickly populated territory where the mound-building tradition was still very much alive. Each town had one or more mounds, on which temples and the dwellings of chiefs and nobles were situated. It seemed quite logical to the Spaniards that these Indians would choose raised sites for their important buildings, and the chroniclers of de Soto's expedition saw nothing remarkable about the mounds, mentioning them only casually. Yet within 250 years some highly learned Americans, unable to believe that the mounds of the Southeast had been built by Indians, were suggesting quite seriously that they were the work of de Soto's own men!

De Soto had served with distinction in the Spanish conquest of Peru. He was one of the few Spaniards to behave honorably during that bloody invasion; he came home from Peru a wealthy man in 1537, and asked Charles V, the Spanish king, for a grant of land in the New World. The king awarded him the governorship of a vaguely defined territory called "Florida," which had been discovered by Ponce de León in 1513 and sketchily explored by several Spanish expeditions in the following two decades.

De Soto collected 622 men, including a Greek engineer, an English longbowman, two Italians, and four "dark men" from Africa, and in April of 1539 they left Cuba for Florida. A month later they reached Tampa Bay, and on May 30 de Soto's soldiers began to go ashore. They were looking for a new kingdom as rich as Peru.

On the first of June they entered an Indian town, called Ucita in the narrative of a member of the expedition known to us only as "the Gentleman of Elvas." This Portuguese knight wrote, "The town was of seven or eight houses, built of timber, and covered with palm-leaves. The chief's house stood near the beach, upon a very high mound made by hand for defense; at the other end of the town was a temple, on the top of which perched a wooden fowl with gilded eyes. . . ." This is the first known description of a mound of the American Indians.

This town had been visited by a band of rough Spaniards eleven years earlier, and the inhabitants did not remember their guests with pleasure. They were no happier with de Soto. He and two of his lieutenants moved into the chief's house; the other dwellings were demolished, as was the temple. De Soto sent scouts inland to survey the territory, and soon smoke signals were rising as the Indians passed the word from village to village that intruders once again had come.

The scouts returned to say that the countryside was a maze of swamps and ponds and marshes; the only routes through the mud were Indian trails so narrow that the Spaniards had been able to travel only two abreast. Worse, the patrol had been ambushed by the Indians; two of the irreplaceable horses had been slain, and several of the men had been wounded.

De Soto would have done well to quit there and return to Spain to enjoy his Peruvian wealth. He would have avoided the torments of a terrible march through 350,000 square miles of unexplored territory, and would have spared himself the early grave he found by the banks of the Mississippi. But a stroke of bad luck in the guise of seeming fortune drew de Soto onward to doom. A marooned Spaniard, a member of an expedition of 1528, appeared; he had lived among the Indians so long, adopting their customs and their language, that he had almost forgotten his former way of life. This man, Juan Ortiz, seemed just what de Soto needed: an interpreter, a guide to the unknown country ahead.

The Spaniards proceeded north, looking for gold. Ortiz spoke to the Indians when he could and arranged peaceful passage through their territory. Where Ortiz could not speak the local language, the Spaniards used cruelty to win their way. The Indians were terrified of the Spanish horses, for they had never seen such animals before. The Spaniards also had packs of ferocious wolfhounds, and were armed with arquebuses. These were clumsy guns that could be fired only once every few minutes—time enough for the Indians to loose dozens of deadly arrows—but the flash and bang and smoke of the guns served to send the native warriors into flight. De Soto enslaved hundreds of Indians,

placing them in irons to carry the baggage. Others he massacred as an example to the tribes ahead, and as the march
continued, the killing increased. In Peru, de Soto had been
generous to the conquered Incas; but here, vexed by the
humid climate and the total lack of treasure, he grew harsh
and stern.

Garcilaso de la Vega, another of the chroniclers of the
expedition, offers much information about the customs of
these Indians. Though not himself an eyewitness, this historian used the accounts of three of de Soto's men for his
book, published in 1605. Garcilaso gives this description
of mound building:

"The Indians of Florida always try to dwell on high
places, and at least the houses of the lords and caciques
[chiefs] are so situated even if the whole village cannot be.
But since all of the land is very flat . . . they build such sites
with the strength of their arms, piling up very large quantities of earth and stamping on it with great force until they
have formed a mound from twenty-eight to forty-two feet
in height. Then on the top of these places they construct
flat surfaces which are capable of holding the ten, twelve,
fifteen or twenty dwellings of the lord and his family and
the people of his service. . . ."

Leading to the houses atop the mounds, says Garcilaso,
"the Indians build two, three or more streets, according to
the number that are necessary, straight up the side of the
hill. These streets are fifteen or twenty feet in width and
are bordered with walls constructed of thick pieces of wood
that are thrust side by side into the earth to a depth of more
than the height of a man. Additional pieces of wood just as
thick are laid across and joined one to the other to form
steps. . . . The steps are four, six or eight feet apart and

their height depends more or less on the disposition and steepness of the hill. Because of the width of these steps, the horses went up and down them with ease. All of the rest of the hill is cut like a wall, so that it cannot be ascended except by the stairs, for in this way they are better able to defend the houses of the lord."

None of the villages had any gold. Each chief told the same story to get rid of the Spaniards: there was a golden land, yes, a village of incredible treasure, quite far away, in another part of the country entirely. De Soto knew they

1   Map of the de Soto explorations.

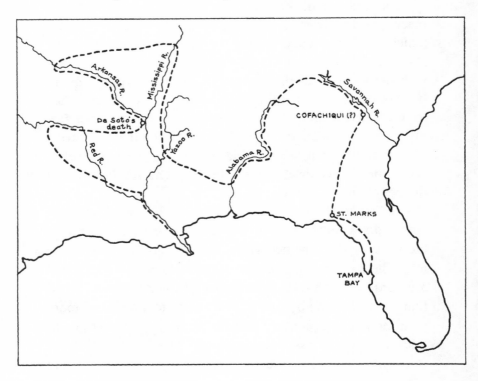

were lying, but there was little he could do save lead his men onward, north along the Florida coast.

On March 3, 1540, they crossed into Georgia. The land, which had been fertile, became a place of dense pine forests where the horses could not enter and hostile Indians lurked. The food supply dwindled; some of the horses died. As they reached northern Georgia, they learned from the natives that they were approaching Cofachiqui, the realm of a fat queen said to be rich in gold. She ruled the area on the South Carolina and Georgia sides of the Savannah River, with her capital near present-day Augusta.

The queen greeted de Soto warmly and presented him with a string of large pearls. He responded by giving her a gold ring set with a ruby. Once the Spaniards were comfortably settled in the town and had dined on turkey and other Indian foods, de Soto brought up the subject of gold and silver. The queen explained that those metals were not mined in her land, but that her people obtained them by trade. She ordered gold and silver brought to de Soto, but what the Indians produced was relatively worthless—copper and thick sheets of mica, which they mistook for the precious metals the Spaniards were after. However, she did have plenty of pearls to offer them. She indicated a temple which, she said, was the burial place of the town's nobility, inviting the Spaniards to loot it and then to search for pearls in a much larger temple in an abandoned town a few miles away.

The Spaniards hurried up the mound to the temple, in which they found the coffins of the nobles and wooden chests containing great quantities of pearls. The Gentleman of Elvas reports that the pearls had been drilled by means of heat, "which causes them to lose their hue," and so had

little value. Discolored or not, they were weighed out; de
Soto's men had taken five hundred pounds of them before
he decided that there was no need to carry such a load on
the rest of their travels. He would, he said, take only fifty
pounds of pearls now, and pick up the rest after he had
finished conquering Florida. But his men insisted on keeping the pearls, and de Soto allowed each of them to take a
double handful.

Now the Spaniards moved on to nearby Talomeco, evac-
uated two years earlier because of a plague. Here too the
chief's house and the temple stood on high artificial mounds.
The temple was 100 feet long and 40 feet wide; within it
were handsomely ornamented idols and numerous chests
of pearls. Enormous bundles of valuable furs were stacked
in rows; adjoining rooms contained weapons that seemed
to be of gold, but which turned out to be merely of copper.
They eyed pearl-decorated broadswords and flawlessly made
bows and arrows likewise set with pearls. Shields of wood,
shields of cowhide, shields of woven cane, all of exquisite
workmanship, delighted them. Even Spaniards who had
beheld the golden riches of Mexico and Peru were awed by
these humbler but no less beautiful objects. But again de
Soto decided to leave behind most of what they had found,
rather than weigh down his men.

Though they still had taken no gold, the Spaniards were
cheerful; after enduring warfare and famine, they had found
a peaceful place where food was plentiful. They hoped to
stay at Cofachiqui at least through the harvest season. But
de Soto had heard of another supposedly wealthy province
twelve days' march ahead, and insisted on searching for it.

On May 3, 1540, the Spaniards left Cofachiqui, forcing
the fat and friendly queen to serve as their guide. She led

the Spaniards to the borders of her territory and gave them the slip in a thicket, taking with her a trunk of perfect pearls that de Soto had coveted. According to legend, one of de Soto's "dark men" helped her escape and took her back to Cofachiqui, where he lived as her husband and co-ruler thereafter.

During the summer of 1540 the Spaniards passed through what one day would be South Carolina, North Carolina, and Tennessee, into the Blue Ridge Mountains. They were disappointed in their hope of treasure, the Indians were more warlike, and the land was agriculturally too poor to support them on their march. They swung south and then southwest, treating the Indians ever more cruelly. In October, they reached south-central Alabama, the country of the Choctaws. De Soto tried to capture their chief, Tuscaloosa, but in the battle that followed 22 Spaniards were slain, 148 (including de Soto) were wounded, and the Spaniards lost many of their spare weapons and much of their gunpowder.

The expedition was crippled. Yet de Soto was unable to admit defeat and instead of withdrawing to the safety of Cuba, forced his men on to new adventures. In March 1541, they again were badly hurt by an Indian attack, losing a dozen men, sixty horses, and many weapons. Still, rumors of gold led them on, and they headed westward. On May 8, 1541, the weary Spaniards came to the Mississippi River a few miles below the present site of Memphis. The river, nearly two miles wide there, amazed them. They spent a tiresome month building barges to ferry themselves across; on the other side were more hostile tribes. Now, in the third year of their quest, the Spaniards drifted on through the Ozarks, across Arkansas, into eastern Oklahoma. They were passing out of the country of the mound-building Indians; now they saw tepee-dwelling nomads on bison-cluttered plains. At last de Soto gave up and ordered his men to turn southeast, toward the Gulf of Mexico. In northern Louisiana, hundreds of miles from the Gulf, he fell ill and died. Another officer took command and led the grieving explorers westward on what he hoped was the overland route to Mexico. Soon they were in the deserts of eastern Texas, facing starvation; doubling back, they came to the Mississippi at the end of 1542, spent a dismal winter there building boats, and in July of 1543 set out down the river. In two weeks, they covered the seven hundred miles to the Gulf,.and kept going towards Mexico. On September 10, 1543, they landed at a Spanish settlement on the Mexican coast, and the long nightmare was over. Amazingly, of the 622 men who had started out with de Soto, 311 survived all the hardships.

3

De Soto's Spaniards had had long exposure to the mound-building Indians of Florida, Georgia, the Carolinas, Tennessee, Arkansas, Alabama, Mississippi, and Louisiana, and the Indians had had a cruel taste of the white man's ways. The next Europeans to arrive in the Southeast were French colonists, who landed in 1562 near the present site of St. Augustine. The colony swiftly failed, and the famine-stricken survivors were rescued by an English ship. A second French expedition arrived in 1564 and was driven out by the Spaniards the following year. In this group was an artist, Jacques Le Moyne, who later produced a series of watercolors depicting Indian life in the Southeast. One of

2   A Florida mound burial. Engraving by De Bry from a
painting by Jacques Le Moyne, sixteenth century.

these showed the Indians mourning at a chief's burial
ground. The mound is no more than a yard high and perhaps two yards across; arrows have been thrust into the
ground around it as a decorative palisade, and a large snail
shell rests at the summit. Le Moyne's caption declares,
"Sometimes the deceased king of this province is buried with
great solemnity, and his great cup from which he was ac-
customed to drink is placed on a tumulus with many arrows
set about it."

Though the mound shown by Le Moyne was small, it
may have been only the core of what was intended as a
full-sized mound. If this is so, Le Moyne's painting is the

first depiction of an Indian burial mound—made while the mound was still in the early stages of construction.

After the departure of the French from Florida, a long silence settled over the mound country. De Soto's men, the first Europeans to see much of the Mississippi Valley, were the last to visit it for at least a century. The next explorers came down the valley from the north.

Frenchmen moving westward along the St. Lawrence River discovered the upper Mississippi in the middle of the seventeenth century. About 1672, France commissioned the explorer Louis Joliet to investigate the Mississippi; he took with him the Jesuit missionary Jacques Marquette, and they embarked down the Mississippi on May 17, 1673. They saw no sign of Indian life on the river until they were as far south as the present site of Quincy, Illinois. There they came upon friendly Indians, visited several villages, and went on.

All about them lay the mounds of the past, but Marquette and Joliet saw none of them. From the river, mounds and embankments would have seemed mere natural formations; they would have had no reason to examine them more closely unless they saw Indian settlements, and there were no settlements. A century and a half later, when this part of the continent was being carved into the farms of white settlers, the evidence of an immense prehistoric population would be found everywhere. But the builders of the valley's thousands of mounds had vanished by 1673, a fact that helped to foster the legend of a lost ancient civilization. Only in the deep South—in Mississippi and Alabama—did the temple-mound people still carry on the old traditions.

The earthworks of the empty North continued to attract

no attention as the eighteenth century dawned; a Jesuit named Jacques Gravier spent the winter of 1700 at an Illinois village he called "Kaowikia"—almost certainly Cahokia— but though he lived among an array of mounds that included one bulkier than Egypt's largest pyramid, he said nothing of them in his journal. He did get as far down the Mississippi as the mouth of the Arkansas River, the point where Marquette and Joliet had turned back; there, Gravier said, was one tribe that had "only one small temple, raised on a mound of earth."

In the early eighteenth century the mound-building tribes of the lower Mississippi were disappearing; speaking of certain Indians of Mississippi, a Frenchman named Bénard de la Harpe noted that their cabins rose "upon mounds of earth made with their own hands, from which it is inferred that these nations are very ancient and were formerly very numerous, although at the present time they hardly number two hundred and fifty persons."

One Southern tribe still living in the old way was carefully studied by Frenchmen who lived among them from 1698 to 1732. These were the Natchez, who at that time numbered about four thousand and lived in seven small villages grouped around an imposing mound 35 feet high. An account by a certain Mathurin La Petit informs us that "the temple of the Natchez in shape resembles an earthen oven over 100 feet in circumference." Le Page du Pratz, who visited the Natchez in 1720, writes that the chief's house stands "upon a mound of earth about eight feet high and sixty feet across." Nine years later the Natchez launched an attack on the French and were nearly exterminated as a result; the few survivors were dispersed among other tribes.

The fortunes of the Southern mound builders were

ebbing, but even in the middle of the eighteenth century there was plenty of evidence that mounds were usual features of Indian life. The Northern mounds were not yet generally known, but it would not have been difficult to assume that they were the work of now-departed tribes of the fifteenth or sixteenth century. One of the earliest notices of Northern mounds appeared in Cadwallader Colden's *History of the Five Nations,* published in 1747, in which he notes that "a round hill" was sometimes raised over a grave in which a corpse had been deposited. He saw nothing extraordinary in this custom.

By now the Thirteen Colonies were firmly established along the Atlantic seaboard, and these English settlements had begun to look toward the unknown wilderness to the west. France and Britain went to war over control of the continent in 1756, and as a result of that war everything east of the Mississippi became British except 2,800 square miles which included the mouth of the river and the town of New Orleans. The way was open for the Thirteen Colonies to sweep westward to the Mississippi, subject only to the objections of the Indian tribes that happened to be in the way. Soon the wagons were rolling through the mountain passes. Soon the forests were falling and the ancient mounds were coming to light. And, not long after, the myth of the Mound Builders was born.

▲▲▲ 2

THE MAKING OF THE MYTH

▲▲▲

The first notices of Northern mounds began to appear in print late in the eighteenth century. On May 3, 1772, a group of Christian Indians led by the missionary David Zeisberger went from western Pennsylvania to found a settlement called Schönbrunn near the present site of New Philadelphia, Ohio. In the course of laying out the town, Zeisberger discovered burial mounds. He mentioned them in his book, *History of the North American Indians*. This was possibly the earliest published account of the Ohio mounds.

Other accounts soon followed. The January 1775 number of the *Royal American Magazine* of Boston ran an article describing and illustrating the extensive earthworks at what would become the town of Circleville, Ohio. A missionary named David Jones, who had seen Ohio mounds in 1772, wrote briefly of them in a book published in 1774. James Adair, whose *History of the American Indians* appeared in 1775, noted that "great mounds of earth, either of a circular or oblong form, having a strong breastwork at a distance around them, are frequently met with."

These early sketchy comments were not accompanied by speculations on lost races. It was generally assumed that the mounds and earthworks had been built by people more advanced than the Ohio Indians of that time, but no one suggested that the builders had not themselves been Indians. However, the mythmakers were beginning to stir. Ezra Stiles, the president of Yale College, heard of the Ohio mounds and asked for more information, thinking he might find evidence for his theory that the American Indians were descended from Canaanites driven from Palestine by

3   The great mound at Marietta. Engraving from *Ancient Monuments of the Mississippi Valley,* by E. G. Squier and E. H. Davis, 1848, from an early painting.

Joshua's army of Israelites. Stiles asked his good friend Benjamin Franklin for an opinion on the mounds; Franklin replied that the earthworks might have been constructed by de Soto in his wanderings.

Meanwhile colonists from New England were settling in Ohio. In 1786 a company was formed to buy Ohio land from the government, and in the winter of 1787–88 emigrants from Massachusetts and Connecticut arrived in the heart of the Ohio mound country and began to build a Yankee village they called Marietta. Its guiding figure was Brigadier General Rufus Putnam, a Revolutionary War veteran. When the settlers laid out their new town, one of their first problems was what to do with the ancient mounds occupying the site.

They were surprisingly reverent toward these monuments of a previous age. General Putnam himself prepared a detailed map of the Marietta earthworks—the first such archaeological map ever made in the United States. The general, who had been trained as a surveyor and military engineer, had earlier chosen the site for the United States Military Academy at West Point and had constructed the fortifications there.

The leaders of the settlement chose to preserve many of the mounds, avenues, and enclosures Putnam had mapped. Three features in particular lay within the area intended to be central Marietta. One was an irregular square enclosure covering about 40 acres and containing four flat-topped pyramids, of which the largest was 188 feet long, 132 feet wide, and 10 feet high. Nearby was a similar square covering 27 acres. To the south stood a mound 30 feet high surrounded by an almost circular wall.

In 1788 it was decided to set aside the two large enclosures and the great mound as public parks. But for this, the Marietta earthworks would surely have been destroyed, as were those in Cincinnati, Circleville, Chillicothe, and many other Ohio cities.

The Reverend Manasseh Cutler, another leader of the Marietta settlement, also carried out important archaeological work. When he arrived in 1788, he found that the dense forest around the mounds was being cut down, and he made counts of the growth rings of the trees. It was already known that each year, as a tree grows, it adds a new ring of wood around its heart; these rings can be seen after the tree is cut down. Cutler counted the rings of some of the trees that had topped the mounds. One tree yielded a count of 463 rings, and near it Cutler saw decayed stumps in which younger trees were growing. This led him to conclude that the mound had been erected no later than the early fourteenth century, and could well be over a thousand years old. Probably never before had tree-ring dating been used on an archaeological site; by this means Cutler helped to establish the fact that the Ohio mounds were not the work of contemporary Indians. (Cutler's figures were not entirely accurate, it turned out; he did not know that some trees add more than one growth ring a year.)

As the migration into Ohio continued, interest in the mounds and their builders became intense—and theories of their origin multiplied. One of the most fertile theorizers of the era was Benjamin Smith Barton of Philadelphia. In 1785, when he was 19, Barton accompanied his uncle, the mathematician and astronomer David Rittenhouse, into the mound country to help lay out the western boundary of Pennsylvania. When not taking part in the work of surveying, Barton would inspect the local geography and geology, study the Indians, and examine the mounds. Two years later he published a little book called *Observations on Some Parts of Natural History,* in which he expressed some ideas on the mounds.

He doubted that the Indians of Ohio had built them. Instead he thought they were the work of Danish Vikings— for, as had already been pointed out, Viking lords were buried in mounds that seemed not very different from those of Ohio. Where had these New World Vikings gone? Why, to Mexico, Barton said. There they had been known as "Toltecs."

The Toltecs were well known to scholars, for the Spanish conquerors of Mexico had heard about them from the defeated Aztecs. According to the Aztecs, the Toltecs had come to Mexico some centuries before the Aztecs themselves had arrived, and for a while had ruled the entire land. Their first great king was Quetzalcoatl, said to be a bearded man of fair skin who was later worshiped as a god in Mexico.

Barton, leaping on the description of Quetzalcoatl as "fair-skinned," argued from that and from the evidence of the mounds that the Mound Builders and the Toltecs were the same people—far-ranging Vikings who had stopped off in the valleys of the Ohio and the Mississippi a thousand or more years ago, before proceeding on to Mexico.

2

While the Ohio mounds were exciting these speculations, more sober investigations were being performed in the Southeast, where de Soto once had roamed. William Bartram, another Philadelphian, carried out a one-man expedition there that won him worldwide fame and provided vivid descriptions of ancient mounds.

Bartram, who lived from 1739 to 1823, was one of seven sons of the famous botanist John Bartram. The elder Bartram had founded a private botanical garden near Philadelphia and earned his living supplying American plants and trees for European gardens. Young William, after several dismal attempts to become a merchant, eventually followed his father into the study of natural history.

Faced with bankruptcy in 1770, William disappeared from Philadelphia and turned up some months later in North Carolina. There he remained, somewhat in disgrace, through 1772. His father urged him to return home and resume his business career; instead, William said, he planned to go as a naturalist to Florida.

John Bartram tried to discourage this "wild notion," but William persevered. He found a London patron, Dr. John Fothergill, who hired him at a salary of £50 a year, plus expenses, to collect plants and mollusks in Florida. "It is a pity that such a genius should sink under distress," Fothergill wrote to John Bartram. Now that the Florida trip was a solid business proposition, the senior Bartram relented and gave it his blessing.

William returned to Philadelphia late in 1772 to plan his journey, and set out on March 20, 1773, beginning four years of wanderings through wild and almost unknown territory. In 1774 and 1775 he shipped specimens, drawings, and journals to Fothergill; the outbreak of the Revolution in 1776 cut off communication between William and his sponsor, but William continued to travel. When he returned from the South in 1777, he settled in Philadelphia and appears not to have left it for the rest of his long life.

Now a celebrity in his own right, he was sought out by every scientist and statesman who came to the city.

His literary masterpiece, *Travels through North & South Carolina, Georgia, East & West Florida . . .* etc. was published in 1791 and was reprinted in many European countries soon thereafter, rapidly becoming established as a classic of American travel writing. His wonderful tales—his meeting with the emperor of the Cherokees; his dinners of venison and fresh trout; his encounters with roaring alligators, graceful cranes, wondrous fishes, otters and frogs, bears and wolves—gave his book a vivid and delightful flavor.

Bartram's chief concern was natural history, but he could not avoid stumbling over mounds everywhere in the South. Early in his book he reports, "evident vestiges of an ancient Indian town may be seen, such as old extensive fields, and conical mounds, or artificial heaps of earth," and similar phrases are frequent in the succeeding five hundred pages.

Late in 1773 Bartram discovered an important mound group on the east side of the Ocmulgee River, opposite the present city of Macon, Georgia. He wrote: "On the heights of these low grounds are yet visible monuments, or traces, of an ancient town, such as artificial mounts or terraces, squares and banks, encircling considerable areas. Their old fields and planting land extend up and down the river, fifteen or twenty miles from the site." Two groups of these mounds still exist and are included in Ocmulgee National Monument; they have come under much study by modern archaeologists.

In Putnam County, Florida, Bartram visited Mount Royal, on the east bank of the St. Johns River, which he and his father had seen while traveling together in 1765. Now, nine years later, he was disturbed to find that the owner of the land had cleared away the handsome groves of orange, palm, and magnolia trees surrounding the mound, in order to plant corn, cotton, and indigo; this plantation had been allowed to run down so that, he said, it now appeared "like a desert, to a great extent, and terminated, on the land side, by frightful thickets, and open pine forests." But the great mound remained.

Other ancient structures were found nearby. On an island in adjoining Lake George, Bartram found "a very pompous Indian mount, or conical pyramid of earth, from which runs in a straight line a grand avenue or Indian highway," and more lay not far away. "This island," he wrote, "appears to have been well inhabited, as is very evident, from the quantities of fragments of Indian earthenware, bones of animals and other remains, particularly in the shelly heights and ridges, all over the island."

Bartram managed to find mounds even by accident. He camped one night a little farther along the St. Johns, and awoke in the morning to find that "I had taken up my lodging on the border of an ancient burying ground. . . . These graves occupied the whole grove, consisting of two or three acres of ground; there were near thirty of these cemeteries of the dead, nearly of an equal size and form, they were oblong, twenty feet in length, ten or twelve feet in width and three or four feet high. . . ." Bartram saw no reason to attribute great antiquity to these burial mounds; he guessed that they were the graves of the victims of a war that had taken place about fifty years before between two Indian tribes.

In September 1774, he visited a Creek Indian town— at the site of the present town of Palatka, Florida—where mound building of a different sort was still being practiced. Here, as in de Soto's time, the Indians observed the custom of placing the important buildings of their village on artificial platforms. The chief entertained Bartram in "a grand, airy pavilion in the center of the village" on such a platform.

Nevertheless, Bartram did not think that *all* the Southeastern mounds were recent. Many were obviously ancient, though he could not know how ancient. When he questioned the Creeks about the mounds, he received vague answers about earlier tribes. One Indian took him to a ruined city near Apalachicola, Florida, where Bartram went among "the mounds or terraces, on which formerly stood their town house or rotunda and square . . . and a little back of this, on a level height or natural step, above the low grounds is a vast artificial terrace or four square mound, now seven or eight feet higher than the common surface of the ground. . . . The Creeks or present inhabitants have a tradition that this was the work of the ancients, many ages prior to their arrival and possessing the country."

Bartram thus carefully distinguished between the mounds the Creeks had built and those built by their unknown predecessors. But his discussion of the mounds was generally overlooked in the nineteenth century, when it was more pleasing to believe that *all* the mounds were the work of extremely ancient races.

The Creeks were one of four similar Southeastern tribes, the others being the Choctaws, Chickasaws, and Cherokees. Bartram believed—incorrectly—that the Cherokees, who lived in the Carolinas, had been pushed out of Georgia and Florida by the arrival of the Creeks. On his way north, therefore, he investigated the possibility that the Cherokees might have built the mounds he had seen in Creek territory.

He found mounds in Cherokee villages, too. "The council or town-house," he wrote, "is a large rotunda, capable of accommodating several hundred people; it stands on the top of an ancient artificial mount of earth, of about twenty feet perpendicular. . . . But it may be proper to observe, that this mount on which the rotunda stands, is of a much ancienter date than the building, and perhaps was raised for another purpose. The Cherokees themselves are as ignorant as we are, by what people or for what purpose these artificial hills were raised; they have various stories concerning them, the best of which amounts to no more than mere conjecture, and leave us entirely in the dark. . . ." Like the Creeks, Bartram learned, the Cherokees claimed to have found the mounds already there when they migrated into the Southeast years before.

One huge structure received special attention from him. This was the great mound in the group later called Rembert's Mounds on the Savannah River in Elbert County, Georgia. Bartram measured it, finding it about 50 feet high and several hundred yards in circumference at the base; a spiral path led up to its flat summit, and on its sides, four niches had been cut out, which he thought had been meant as resting places or lookout posts. Bartram's description of this major temple mound is particularly valuable, for the mound no longer exists; a flood carried most of it away in 1908, and archaeologists visiting the site forty years later found nothing but a stump four feet high. Although he believed that the mound was the work of some early Indian tribe, he was puzzled by the reason for its existence: "It is altogether unknown to us," he wrote, "what could have induced the Indians to raise such a heap of earth in this place. . . . It is reasonable to suppose, however, that [such mounds] were to serve some important purpose in those days, as they were public works, and would have required the united labour and attention of a whole nation. . . ."

Bartram belonged to the conservative school of thought in the mound controversy. At no point did he speak of Toltecs, Vikings, or other imagined non-Indian Mound Builders. In the closing pages of his *Travels* he summed up his ideas about the Southeastern mounds and their creators, saying that before the Creeks and Cherokees arrived, "all that country was probably many ages preceding . . . inhabited by one nation or confederacy, who were ruled by the same system of laws, customs and language; but so ancient, that the Cherokees, Creeks, or the nation they conquered, could render no account for what purpose these monuments were raised." It was Bartram's guess that some of the mounds had been lookout towers, some were the foundations of fortresses, some had served "for ornament and recreation," and some as "high places for sacrifice." He was quite careful to avoid inventing great imaginary civilizations as builders of the mounds.

Another cautious observer of the Southern mounds was Thomas Jefferson. In 1787, writing of mounds in a letter to a friend, Jefferson declared, "It is too early to form theories on those antiquities, we must wait with patience till more facts are collected."

Jefferson, a man of broad scientific interests, had studied the American Indians since his boyhood and ranked as one of his era's outstanding experts on them. He had personally excavated an Indian mound in his native Virginia and described this archaeological project in the only book he ever published, *Notes on the State of Virginia,* which appeared in 1785. His account of his mound excavation shows that

Jefferson regarded the burial mounds of Virginia, at least, as the work of Indians, and shows also that he was far ahead of his time in an understanding of the true aims of archaeology. In Jefferson's day and for almost a century thereafter, the goal of most archaeologists was to unearth attractive ancient treasures, and they dug quickly and carelessly to reach the buried hoards. Gradually, professional archaeologists came to realize the importance of recording all the seemingly minor features of a site so that they could eventually reconstruct a full picture of a civilization even to small details. Jefferson understood the value of this method, and the detailed report on his mound work in Virginia is often regarded as the first truly scientific archaeological publication in the New World.

4

Descriptions of mounds and their contents now began to appear frequently in the scholarly journals of the young republic. Many towns were being founded in the Ohio Valley and along the Ohio's tributaries, the Miami, Scioto, and Muskingum rivers; each townsite had its mounds, and generally each town had its antiquarian who studied them before they were swept away by progress. Cincinnati was settled in 1788; soon came Athens, Manchester, Chillicothe, Portsmouth, and a dozen more, all having mounds.

Cincinnati's mounds were explored in 1794 by Colonel Winthrop Sargent, who took a number of artifacts from a mound at the intersection of Third and Main streets. He published his findings in 1799 in the *Transactions of the American Philosophical Society,* the journal of a Philadelphia group that had a keen interest in the mounds.

The English astronomer Francis Baily, accompanying a party of settlers down the Ohio River in 1796, stopped to examine a group of mounds on what is today the West Virginia side of the river, and wrote the first recorded notice of the striking Grave Creek Mound, which had already been discovered and partly excavated by unknown pioneers. The mounds, Baily wrote, must have been "built by a race of people more enlightened than the present Indians, and at some period of time very far distant; for the present Indians know nothing about their use, nor have they any tradition concerning them."

Several other accounts of mounds appeared at about the same time. Shortly after the turn of the century there appeared two papers that were of particular importance for they represented the positions of the two main factions in the developing Mound Builder controversy.

The first was the work of the Right Reverend James Madison, the first Protestant Episcopal Bishop of Virginia. In 1803, he published in the *Transactions of the American Philosophical Society* an essay entitled "The Supposed Fortifications of the Western Country." In this paper he dismissed the various lost-race theories of Mound Builders and asserted that the mounds and other earthworks had been built by the ancestors of the Indians who currently lived in the mound regions.

Two years later a New England minister, the Reverend Thaddeus M. Harris, published his book, *Journal of a Tour into the Territory Northwest of the Alleghany Mountains.* He had visited Ohio in 1803, spending much of his time examining the Marietta mounds, and had concluded that the earthworks were too elaborate an engineering feat to have been the work of mere savage Indians. They must have been created, he argued, by some "higher" race, and he revived Barton's notion that the Mound Builders were the Toltecs of Mexican tradition. (He did not, like Barton, claim that the two groups were descended from Vikings; he suggested only that this noble mound-building civilization lived in the Ohio Valley at some early date, ultimately moving on to Mexico and being replaced by Indians in the North.)

Neither Madison's opinions nor those of Harris were new, but the two men came to stand for the opposing schools of thought. The lost-race supporters lined up behind Harris, and the skeptics behind Madison.

Bringing the Toltecs back into the discussion renewed a debate that had been going on for several centuries, ever since the Spaniards had discovered the high civilization of Mexico and Peru. The cities of the Aztecs and the Incas were in some respects grander and more advanced than those of sixteenth-century Europe, a fact that persuaded some theorists that their builders could not possibly have been native to the Americas. No, they must have come from the Old World, settling among the red-skinned savages and erecting their great cities. But where had the ancestors of the Aztecs and Incas come from, and how long ago? Were they of Phoenician descent? Did they come from the supposed lost continent of Atlantis? Were they Greeks? Persians? Hindus? Vikings? For that matter, how had the red-skinned savages themselves—the ordinary "Indians"— come to America?

No people, civilized or savage, could be considered native to the Americas by those who took the Bible literally. The Bible spoke of just one act of creation, which took place in the Garden of Eden. Eden was thought to be in

Asia, and Asia must thus have been the homeland of America's red men, as it was of all human beings.

Long before anything was known about the geography of western North America, the idea had been put forward that the Indians must have crossed to the New World out of eastern Asia at some point where Old World and New were close together or actually joined. The physical resemblance of the American Indians to the natives of eastern Asia helped to support this theory, which first emerged in the late sixteenth century. In the first half of the eighteenth century, the explorer Vitus Bering gave strength to the theory by discovering a 56-mile-wide strait separating Alaska from Siberia. This discovery of what is now known as the Bering Strait put an end to discussion of how the Indians had reached the New World; by the late eighteenth century it was generally agreed that they had come out of Asia via the Bering Strait, either by boat or in the winter over a bridge of ice, and then had spread throughout the two Americas. This theory is still universally accepted.

But some natives of the American continents were clearly more advanced than others, and European thinkers long wondered about the origins of such civilizations as those of the Aztecs, the Mayas, and the Incas. The most persistent notion was that the Indians—or at least the most intelligent Indians—were descended from the Ten Lost Tribes of Israel.

The Bible tells how, after the death of King Solomon, the twelve Hebrew tribes divided into two kingdoms, Israel in the northern part of Palestine, Judah in the south. Both kingdoms had their troubles, but Israel in particular developed a tendency to slip back into idol-worship; despite the warnings of their prophets, the Israelites "built them

high places [mounds?] in all their cities," as we learn in II
Kings, 17: "And they set them up images and groves in
every high hill, and under every green tree: And there they
burnt incense in all the high places, as did the heathen. . . ."
Eventually God showed His displeasure by letting the blood-
thirsty Assyrians defeat the Israelites and carry them off
into captivity, the climax coming in 722 B.C. when Sargon
of Assyria captured Israel's capital and took 27,290 of its
inhabitants into slavery. Eventually the kingdom of Judah
also fell, and its people went into exile in Babylonia, but
these Hebrews were later allowed to return to Palestine. Of
the vanished ten northern tribes nothing more was heard.

In the sixteenth century Diego de Landa, a Spanish priest
serving in Mexico, put together a book of tales told to
him by the Mayas, in which he wrote: "Some of the old
people of Yucatán say that they have heard from their ancestors that this land was occupied by a race of people, who
came from the East and whom God had delivered by opening twelve paths through the sea. If this were true, it necessarily follows that all the inhabitants of the Indies are the
descendants of the Jews. . . ."

The idea became widespread and popular. Many books
were published in the seventeenth and eighteenth centuries
to "prove" that the Indians were the Ten Lost Tribes of
Israel. William Penn believed it and said that Indians reminded him very strongly of the Jews of London. The most
dedicated of the "Lost Tribesmen" was an eccentric Irish
nobleman, Lord Kingsborough, who in the 1830's published
nine huge volumes on the subject; he went bankrupt doing
it and died in a debtors' prison.

Many scholars were tempted to link the "high places" of
Israel with the mounds of North America. And so, while the

legend of a great lost race of Mound Builders was taking form in the first two decades of the nineteenth century, that race was often given an Israelite ancestry. In 1820, for example, Caleb Atwater of Ohio—one of the important early figures in American archaeology—compared the "high places" and the mounds, observing that on the high places of Palestine "great national affairs were transacted. Here they crowned and deposed their kings; here they concluded peace and declared war. Here the nation assembled at stated seasons, to perform the solemn worship of their deities. Here they celebrated anniversaries of great national events. . . ."

Let the reader examine the mounds of Ohio, Atwater wrote, "and then ask himself, Whether those who raised our monuments, were not originally from Asia? . . . examine the loftiest mounds [in Ohio], and compare them with those described as being in Palestine. Through the wide world, such places seem to have been preferred by the men of ancient times who erected them."

To be fair to Atwater, he should not really be placed in the group that advocated the Ten Lost Tribes theory. As we shall soon see, he thought that the Mound Builders were a non-Indian race from Asia, similar in culture to the Hebrews of Palestine, but he does not actually claim they were the uprooted victims of the Assyrians; at another point in his book he suggests that the Mound Builders reached North America "as early as the days of Abraham and Lot"—that is, more than a thousand years before the Assyrians invaded Israel.

Others were less cautious. They wrote enthusiastically about the Hebrew migration to the Americas, turning out detailed but fantastic essays giving the dates of arrival, the

routes taken by specific tribes, and the mounds erected by
each. These books were widely read, and their authors often
won brief but dazzling fame.

Few voices now were heard to claim that the mounds
were the work of Indians. In 1811, the highly respected
DeWitt Clinton, Mayor of New York, examined the
mounds of western New York State and announced that
their builders had been Vikings. Many agreed, and Clinton
repeated his statement in following years.

In 1819 John Heckewelder, a missionary who had lived
among the Delaware Indians since 1772, published a book
on the Indians of his region that introduced a new twist
to the mound story. Heckewelder set down a tale told to
him by the Delawares, also known as the Lenni-Lenape
Indians, describing how they had come to their part of the
country from the West. After a long journey they reached
the Mississippi and sent scouts across who returned with the
news "that the country east of the Mississippi was inhabited
by a very powerful nation who had many large towns. . . ."
These people, Heckewelder said, were called the *Alligewi*
or *Tallegewi*. "Many wonderful things are told of [them],"
he wrote. "They are said to have been remarkably tall and
stout, and there is a tradition that there were giants among
them. . . . It is related that they had built to themselves
regular fortifications or intrenchments," some of which
Heckewelder himself had seen. One was on the Huron
River, six or eight miles from Lake Erie; it consisted of two
walls of earth with a deep ditch on one side and, nearby,
"a number of large flat mounds." Heckewelder relates how
the Lenape allied themselves with another tribe called the
Mengwe and made war against the Alligewi; ". . . great

battles were fought in which many warriors fell on both sides. The enemy fortified their large towns and erected fortifications, especially on large rivers and near lakes. . . ." In one battle "hundreds fell, who were afterwards buried in holes or laid together in heaps and covered over with earth. No quarter was given, so that the Alligewi at last, finding that their destruction was inevitable if they persisted in their obstinacy, abandoned the country to the conquerors and fled down the Mississippi River, from whence they never returned."

No one doubted that the old missionary had really heard such tales from the Indians, and, since Heckewelder had collected these stories in the 1770's before most of the Ohio mounds and fortifications had been discovered, it could not be said that he was concocting a legend to fit an existing theory. Those who wanted to believe that the builders of the mounds were the ancestors of contemporary Indians used the Heckewelder story as proof that the Alligewi or Tallegewi were really the Cherokees. They based this partly on the supposed similarity between the names "Tallegewi" and "Chellakee," an alternate form of "Cherokee." They drew on Cherokee myths, which told how they had lived in the north before settling in the Carolinas. And they pointed to the evidence that the Cherokees were builders of mounds, ignoring the Cherokees' own admission that they built their important lodges on top of mounds left by an unknown earlier people. By carefully selecting the facts, it was possible to "prove" that the Cherokees had built the mounds of the Ohio Valley, then had been invaded by an alliance of the Delawares and the Iroquois (the Lenape and the Mengwe), and had built most of the Ohio embankments as defenses in that war; finally the Cherokees were defeated and fled to the Southeast, their lands being divided between the two conquering tribes.

But Heckewelder had also spoken of the Alligewi as "giants." The Cherokees were not giants, nor were any other Indian tribes; and so the old missionary's story touched off a search for a race of giant Mound Builders in the Ohio Valley.

Few people wanted to believe that the Indians had built the mounds. The myth of the Mound Builders was a satisfying one; it was splendid to dream of a lost prehistoric race in the heart of America; if the vanished ones had been giants, or white men, or Israelites, or Toltecs, or Vikings, or giant white Jewish Toltec Vikings, so much the better. The United States was then busy fighting an undeclared war against the Indians, who blocked their path to expansion; the Indians were being pushed out of their territory, imprisoned, forced to migrate, or simply massacred; and as this century-long campaign of genocide proceeded, it may have been comforting for the conquerors to imagine that there once had been another race that these Indians had pushed out in the same way. Consciences might ache a bit over the uprooting of the Indians, but not if it could be shown that the Indians, far from being 'long-established settlers in the land, were themselves mere intruders who had brutally shattered the glorious old Mound Builder civilization.

A few quiet scholars heeded Jefferson's advice, and went about the job of digging up mounds and examining their contents without seeking to create myths. One of them was Dr. J. H. McCulloh, Jr., of Baltimore, who examined the Ohio mounds and published three essays on them between

1813 and 1829. After careful study, McCulloh concluded that the Indians of the Americas all belonged to the same race, although there were sharp local variations in looks and culture; and this race, he said, comprised the first human settlers of the New World. He felt no need to invent an earlier race of Mound Builders to account for the antiquities found in North America.

But McCulloh was ahead of his time. In the early nineteenth century, people interested in the mounds preferred to put their faith in the fantastic myths.

▲▲▲ 3

THE TRIUMPH OF THE MYTH

▲▲▲

One of the first organizations in the United States devoted to archaeological studies was the American Antiquarian Society, founded in Boston in 1812. Its members were particularly interested in the Ohio mounds, which seemed to hold such marvels and mysteries. When the society published its first volume of archaeological essays in 1820, much of the book was devoted to a long work entitled "Description of the Antiquities Discovered in the State of Ohio and other Western States," by Caleb Atwater, the postmaster of Circleville, Ohio.

Atwater, who lived from 1778 to 1867, grew up among the Ohio mounds and studied them nearly all his life, even as they vanished with the spread of civilization. His own town of Circleville, founded in 1806, was laid out following the outlines of two circular earthworks, the outer one a thousand feet in diameter. These became Circle Street and Circle Alley, but when Atwater wrote his essay in 1820 he noted that the earthen walls, only five or six feet high, "are disappearing before us daily, and will soon be gone." (Nothing remains of them today, nor anything of Circleville's original town layout.) Diligently Atwater toured all of Ohio,

50

describing and surveying the prehistoric earthworks that were then succumbing to progress. His essay provides unique data on the state of these monuments just before they vanished forever. Atwater's conclusion—"that the works described in this publication were erected by a race of men widely different from any tribe of North American Indians known in modern times"—was wrong; but his work is nevertheless a landmark in the history of American archaeology, being the first serious and detailed study of the antiquities of a single region.

In his opening pages Atwater adopts a sober tone. He scoffs at the "crude and indigested statements" of those who dash off theories "after having visited a few ancient works," and mocks those who conclude from a single example that all the earthworks were devoted to sun worship or were military forts. He also points out that the presence of supposed Roman coins in various mounds proved nothing, since the coins could have been brought to the New World long after Columbus's voyage.

Atwater divides New World antiquities into three classes. The first comprises things produced by the North American Indians; he dismisses these as "neither numerous nor very interesting. They consist of rude stone axes and knives, of pestles used in preparing maize for food, of arrowheads," and other humble products of "men in a savage state, little versed in the arts of civilized life. . . ."

The second class of antiquities consists of those brought by people of European origin: coins, medals, knives, guns, and other objects scattered through the Ohio Valley by the French explorers and soldiers of the seventeenth and eighteenth centuries. Atwater brushes aside the possibility that European seafarers before Columbus visited the Americas.

The third "and most highly interesting" class of antiquities, according to Atwater, is the one "belonging to that people who erected our ancient forts and tumuli."[1] He declares that the Ohio earthworks were built by a people far more civilized than the Indians, although less advanced than Europeans.

He provides a detailed description, accompanied by charts, of many important Ohio earthworks that no longer exist, or that survive only in fragmentary form. Atwater starts with the earthworks of Newark, Ohio, which have survived better than most, though probably he would be surprised to find that Newark's large eight-sided "fort" and its adjoining circular enclosure today are part of a municipal golf course. The octagon in his day covered some 40 acres, with walls about 10 feet high. Eight openings 15 feet wide pierced the walls, with a small mound of earth in front of each. Nearby was the 22-acre circular "fort," and at a greater distance was another large circular enclosure with a square "fort" beside it. Atwater felt that all of these were structures meant for defense.

Next he turns to the Marietta earthworks, expressing his pleasure that "no despoiling hand has been laid upon them," and quotes several accounts of them, including one by the Marietta physician, Samuel Hildreth, who had dug at Marietta in the spring of 1819. Noting that some writers had been puzzled because no Mound Builder tools had ever been found, Atwater himself observes that if the Marietta earthworks had been built with the aid of iron shovels, these would long ago have rusted away; and in any case, he writes, "with shovels made of wood, earth enough to have constructed these works might have been taken from the sur-

[1] *Tumulus* is Latin for "mound."

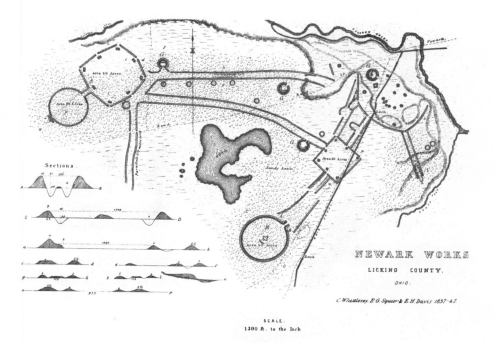

4   Diagram of the Newark works. Squier and Davis, 1848.

face, with as much ease, almost, as if they were made of iron." Atwater's belief that the Mound Builders had probably used wooden spades and shovels is clearly enough stated here. Yet this passage was conveniently overlooked or misinterpreted in later years by those who used other sections of Atwater's text to "prove" that he and Dr. Hildreth had found iron tools and even steel swords in the Ohio mounds.

Atwater gives a good deal of space to the earthworks of his own town of Circleville, describing the double circular enclosure that gave the town its name, and several others,

which he predicts "will entirely disappear in a few years."
He is particularly impressed by the geometrical regularity
of the main Circleville enclosures—circles and squares constructed with such accuracy that they seemed to indicate
that the builders had been master surveyors; ". . . the measurement was much more correct," Atwater writes, "than it
would have been, in all probability, had the present inhabitants undertaken to construct such a work. Let those consider this circumstance, who affect to believe these antiquities
were raised by the ancestors of the present race of Indians."

After discussing several other groups of Ohio embankments and fortifications, Atwater turns to a consideration of
Ohio's burial mounds. The first ones he discusses are those
of Cincinnati, now long gone. He gives special attention to
a mound at Third and Main Streets which had been excavated twice, in 1794 and 1815. The first time, the mound's
explorer had found artifacts of stone and bone in it, some
of them carved with "hieroglyphics" and the sculptured representation of a fierce bird. He had also discovered some
lumps of lead ore and a sheet of copper. When the mound
was re-entered 21 years later, it proved to contain several
dozen human skeletons, a number of beads, some large seashells cut to serve as eating utensils, and a few mysterious
objects made of copper in the form of little curved plates
connected by hollow rods.

These were exciting finds, for they gave evidence that the
Mound Builders had been users of metal, and reinforced the
belief in their superiority to ordinary savage Indians. But
Atwater was able to cite an even more spectacular discovery, that his friend Samuel Hildreth, the Marietta doctor,
had made in a Marietta burial mound in the summer of
1819. Next to a skeleton, Hildreth had found three cup-

shaped objects 2¼ inches across which he thought were
ornaments for a shield or a belt; they were made of copper
overlaid with a thick plate of silver. Nearby was a 6-inch-
long piece of silver that appeared to be the upper part of a
sword scabbard. Some broken pieces of copper tube filled
with iron rust were also found; Hildreth guessed that they
were from the lower end of the scabbard. No sword was
found. From the size of the trees growing on top of the
mound, Hildreth estimated that it could not be less than
five hundred years old.

The metal objects found at Cincinnati and Marietta took
their place in the growing Mound Builder myth. Again and
again they were cited as proof of the technological superiority of this vanished race. For a while some archaeologists
believed that the copper and the silver of the Marietta objects had been joined by the difficult process of plating,
which only an advanced civilization would be familiar with.
The idea that the Mound Builders were expert metallurgists
was not disproved for decades.

Atwater himself had found some metal artifacts in a large
Circleville mound "which the ruthless hand of man is de-
stroying." Near two skeletons he discovered a plate of rusted
metal which seemed to resemble cast iron, and a handle
made of elk's horn, at one end of which were traces of rust
indicating the onetime presence of the iron blade of a sword
or large knife. Later, those who read Atwater carelessly or
relied on third-hand information began to circulate the notion that he had found a steel sword and a piece of cast iron
in the Circleville mound. His own report said nothing of
the kind, but the story, once it got around, was difficult to
squelch. The metal in the Circleville mound was probably
raw meteoric iron, not cast at all—but somehow men trans-

formed it into proof of Mound Builder greatness.

For mounds outside the State of Ohio, Atwater had to rely on the accounts of other travelers, such as H. H. Brackenridge, whose paper, "On the population and tumuli of the aborigines of North America," had appeared in the *Transactions of the American Philosophical Society* in 1818. Brackenridge had pointed out that the mounds along the lower Mississippi were different in shape and size from most of those of Ohio, being much larger and flat on top. Among the mounds he mentions are those at St. Louis, the Cahokia mounds in western Illinois, and others in Mississippi, Louisiana, and Arkansas. "I have been sometimes induced to think," Brackenridge had written, "that, at the period when these were constructed, there was a population as numerous as that which once animated the borders of the Nile, or of the Euphrates, or of Mexico. . . . I am perfectly satisfied that cities, similar to those of ancient Mexico, of several hundred thousand souls, have existed in this country."

2

As a surveyor of mounds Atwater was methodical, careful, and reasonably accurate. He was more of a romantic when it came to offering explanations and theories. Who built the mounds? Where did they come from? When did they come to the United States? Where did they go? Atwater examines various possibilities, citing such things as the Palestinian worship of hills and mountains—the Biblical "high places"—and the pyramids of Egypt and Mexico, as well as the burial mounds and earthworks of the ancient inhabitants of Britain and the cone-shaped mounds of earth a traveler in Russia had recently found over a wide area.

From these various items Atwater constructed a theory of the mounds based on the concept that all human cultures radiated from one place: the point at which Noah's Ark came to rest in the mountains of Armenia after the Deluge. The descendants of Noah, according to Atwater, spread out via Russia, some going westward in Europe as far as the British Isles, others going eastward into Asia.

One of the great debates among modern historians is "diffusionism" versus "independent invention"—that is, whether cultural similarities between remote parts of the world are the result of vast migrations of people or ideas, or simply the outcome of separate but similar thoughts. Atwater was a super-diffusionist. He claimed that rivers in Britain and Russia have the same names; that ancient Russian pottery is similar to that found in burial mounds in Scotland and Ohio; that the existence of mounds in far-flung parts of the world proves a common ancestry for mankind. He lumps together structures as different in form as the pointed pyramids of Egypt, the flat-topped pyramids of Mexico, the stone burial mounds of ancient Europe, the conical mounds of Ohio, and the flat-topped earthen mounds of the lower Mississippi, and finds a common denominator in the mere fact that all are mounds of one sort or another. In passing, he takes aim at the idea that America's Mound Builders could have been the ancestors of the American Indians. He cannot believe that the sad and demoralized Indians of the Ohio of his time could ever have had the skills required to build the mounds. "Have our present race of Indians ever buried their dead in mounds?" he asks. "Have they constructed such works as are described in the preceding pages? Were they acquainted with the use of silver, or iron, or copper?"

But what was the route of the Mound Builders on their journey from Noah's Mount Ararat to southern Ohio?

Atwater did not think that the mound-building concept came across the Atlantic from Western Europe. He traced the route the other way around the world, from Asia into Alaska via the Bering Strait. Out of Siberia, he said, came savage Asian hunters, who became the ancestors of the American Indian; but by the same route also came more civilized shepherds and farmers from India, China, and Russia, who built the American mounds.

India, Atwater thought, was the chief source of the Mound Builders. He deduced this from certain parallels of custom: "The temples, altars, and sacred places of the Hindoos," he notes, "were always situated on the bank of some stream of water. The same observation applies to the temples, altars, and sacred places of those who erected our tumuli." In addition Atwater offers the evidence of a three-headed "idol"—actually a pot—found in Tennessee. "Does it not represent the three chief gods of India—Brahma, Vishnoo, and Siva?" he asks. "All I pretend to do," he declares, "is to lay an unvarnished statement of facts before the reader, who can form what opinion he chooses on the subject."

When did they come to Ohio, then?

"It was in an early age of the world," replies Atwater. He compares the antiquities of Rome—paved roads, stone aqueducts, marble statues, stately palaces—with the humble earthen heaps of Ohio. He points out the stone axes, the mica mirrors, the simple pottery of America's ancient inhabitants. So clearly the migration occurred long ago, perhaps quite soon after the Ark itself came to rest—"as early as the days of Abraham and Lot," perhaps. The Ohio earthworks must have been built long before Rome was founded, he argued, since the artifacts found in them were so much cruder than those of Rome. Nor could the Lost Tribes of Israel have built the mounds; by the time of the Assyrian conquest of Israel in 722 B.C., the world had attained a higher degree of civilization than was found in the mounds.

In Atwater's time, most religious people believed that the world had been created in 4004 B.C. and that Noah's Deluge had happened in 2349 B.C. These figures had been calculated by a seventeenth-century Irish clergyman, James Ussher, who simply added up the ages of all Biblical characters back to Adam. The legendary date of the founding of Rome is 753 B.C. Sometime between 2349 and 753 B.C., then, the Mound Builders had crossed out of Asia into the New World, Atwater thought.

He saw the movement of the Mound Builders through North America as slow and marked by steady progress. The proof of this, he said, is in the mounds themselves. Those in the North, along the Great Lakes, are relatively few in number and small in size, but the mounds become more numerous and much larger to the south. The Mound Builders' population "must have wonderfully increased as they slowly descended the water courses, and their improvement in the useful arts is every where visible."

He adds, "That they lived here for a long time, appears evident from the very numerous cemeteries, and the vast numbers of persons of all ages who were here buried. It is highly probable that more persons were buried in these mounds than now live in this state." He wrote at a time when Ohio's population was about 700,000. Atwater correctly saw that such elaborate earthworks must have been the products of a dense population well supplied with food.

A sparse tribe of huntsmen, preoccupied with the need simply to keep alive, could never have built them.

Atwater did not think that these populous and civilized Mound Builders had been driven out of Ohio by savages. The fortifications were indications that they had experienced attack, but he argued that they must have moved out voluntarily and in a leisurely way. The migration from Ohio took place at least a thousand years ago, he asserted, taking into consideration the tree-ring counts.

Where did the Mound Builders go?

Clearly to Mexico. "Our ancient works," he wrote, "continue all the way into Mexico, increasing indeed in size, number, and grandeur, but preserving the same forms. . . . The form of our works is round, square, semicircular, octagonal, &c., agreeing in all these respects with the works in Mexico." The fact that Mexico's temples were of stone and those of Ohio were of earth seemed to him simply an improvement in building techniques.

It was a neat, clear, and—given the incomplete knowledge of the day—reasonably convincing theory. Against some of the wild and woolly notions of his era, Atwater seems the voice of reason itself as he traces his Hindu shepherds across the face of North America and down the valley of the Mississippi into Mexico. Since most of the continent west of the Mississippi was unexplored, he had no way of knowing that the trail of mounds from Alaska to the Great Lakes was nonexistent, or that there was another large gap in the evidence of migration between the Gulf Coast and the centers of Mexican civilization. The idea that mounds could be found everywhere, from the place where Noah's Ark came to rest to the capital of the Aztecs, was a myth; but Caleb Atwater deserves the respect due a pioneer, even if

his conclusions did not live up to the breadth and depth of
his researches.

3

Atwater's thorough study of the Ohio mounds had two
immediate successors, both the work of men who also were
eminent public figures not noted for bizarre speculations.
Each made an important contribution to American archaeology, though both were tinged at least in part by the at-
mosphere of fantasy then shrouding the mounds.

The first was William Henry Harrison, best known to us
as the man who served as President for the shortest time.
(Harrison, the ninth President, died in 1841 after just one
month in office.) Born in Virginia in 1773, he hoped to be
a doctor, but entered the army at the age of 18 after his
father's death. As a young officer, he was sent to Ohio in
1791 to help crush an uprising of the Indians; in the course
of this warfare he saw a good deal of the mound country.
Later he served as governor of the Indiana Territory, as a
military leader in the War of 1812, as a member from Ohio
of the House of Representatives, as United States Senator,
and as minister to Colombia. When he returned from Colombia in 1829, he went into temporary retirement in Ohio,
though he was soon active in politics again, running for
President unsuccessfully in 1836 and winning in 1840.

Although he liked to pretend he was a simple backwoods-
man, Harrison was actually a man of culture and attain-
ment. Archaeological matters were of high interest to him;
during his years of temporary political inactivity he devoted
a good deal of study to the earthworks near his Ohio home,
and in 1832 he presented his theories about the mounds in

an address before the Historical Society of Ohio.

Harrison's approach was basically romantic. He saw the mounds as relics of a great race; he imagined stirring battles, sweeping migrations of tribes under attack, mighty swarms of civilized people streaming through the heartland of what one day would be the United States of America. To learn of them, he wrote, "we must search amidst the remains which are still before us. . . . We learn first, from the extensive country covered by their remains, that they were a numerous people. Secondly, that they were congregated in considerable cities. . . . Thirdly, that they were essentially an agricultural people; because, collected as they were in great numbers, they could have depended on the chase [hunting] but for a small portion of their subsistence." He was of the opinion that the Mound Builders "were compelled to fly from a more numerous or a more gallant people. No doubt the contest was long and bloody. . . ." The attackers, he thought, came from both the north and the south, and the Mound Builders made their last stand on the banks of the Ohio River; ". . . it was here that a feeble band was collected . . . to make a last effort for the country of their birth, the ashes of their ancestors, and the altars of their gods. That the crisis was met with fortitude, and sustained with valor, need not be doubted. . . . But their efforts were in vain, and flight or death were the sad alternatives. . . ."

Harrison says little about the conquerors of the Mound Builders, other than to state that in the valley of the Ohio "there are indubitable marks of its being thickly inhabited by a race of men, inferior to the authors of the great works we have been considering, after the departure of the latter. Upon many places, remains of pottery, pipes, stone hatchets and other articles, are found in great abundance, which are evidently of inferior workmanship to those of the former people."

This was a useful contribution to archaeological thought. The Ohio Valley had been occupied only by nomadic hunting tribes when the American settlers arrived in the 1780's; Harrison apparently was the first to point out that between the end of the mound-building period and the appearance of the Indian hunters there probably had been a group of farming Indians in the valley who stood midway between the glories of the Mound Builders and the savagery of the eighteenth-century tribesmen.

In the matter of where the Mound Builders had gone, Harrison followed what was becoming the standard theory: that they had emigrated to Mexico. "The pictural records of that nation," he wrote, "ascribe their origin to the Astecks, a people who are said to have arrived first in Mexico about the middle of the Seventh century.[2] An American author, the Rt. Rev. Bishop Madison, of Virginia, having with much labor investigated this subject, declares his conviction that these Astecks are one and the same people with those who once inhabited the valley of the Ohio. . . ."

Another brilliant analysis of the mounds was produced about the same time as Harrison's by Albert Gallatin (1761–1849), the Swiss-born economist who was Thomas Jefferson's Secretary of the Treasury. After a long career in public office, Gallatin had become a banker in 1827 and in his later years concerned himself largely with the study of American Indians. In 1836 he published an important work on the Indians, and six years later he founded and became

[2] Modern archaeologists place the arrival of the Aztecs in Mexico in the thirteenth century.

the first president of the American Ethnological Society.
His final contribution to his chosen science was a pioneering
essay on American Indian languages, published in 1848,
when he was 87 years old.

In his public career Gallatin was cool and prudent, somewhat conservative of thought, and immune to popular delu-
sions and fantasies. Much the same attitude can be seen in
the discussion of mounds that he included in his 1836 book
on the Indians. Pointing out that the Indians themselves
seemed to know nothing about the mounds, he nevertheless
declared, "There is nothing in their construction or the
remnants which they contain indicative of a much more advanced state of civilization than that of the present inhabitants." He cautioned that too little was known about the
mounds or the Indians to permit real understanding of their
history. But he went so far as to guess that the mounds
"were the work of a more populous nation than any now
existing," one that had a well-developed agricultural system.

The large flat-topped mounds, of which the Cahokia
Mound near East St. Louis, Illinois, was then the best-
known example, struck Gallatin as having "a strong family
likeness to the Mexican pyramids." The earthen ramparts
and embankments of Ohio puzzled him, though, for they
were unlike any fortifications constructed by existing Indian
tribes. This led him to suggest that they were the work of a
race different from contemporary Indians, perhaps influenced by the great civilizations of Mexico.

Unlike Harrison, Gallatin did not think that the Mound
Builders had migrated south to Mexico to create those great
civilizations. Instead, he felt that Mexican ideas must have
drifted northward and been adopted by the people of the
Mississippi Valley. Some of the arguments he produced

to support this idea turned out afterward to be incorrect; but by suggesting that the mounds of Ohio were the work of prehistoric farmers under the influence of Mexico, he provided one of the foundations for later understanding of the mound-building phenomenon.

4

When we turn from Atwater, Harrison, and Gallatin to some of their contemporaries, we find ourselves in a very different realm. We meet a group of flamboyant, imaginative writers of pseudo-history who did not hesitate to churn out fantastic tales of the Mound Builders. The myth of the mounds had caught the public fancy, and what delighted the public most keenly was the image of a great empire dragged down to destruction by hordes of barbarians.

The first of these stirring accounts of the downfall of the Mound Builders appeared in 1795; dozens followed, of which the most successful was Josiah Priest's *American Antiquities and Discoveries in the West,* published in 1833. It sold 22,000 copies within thirty months, a gigantic number for those days. Priest gave his readers what they were looking for. "Ancient millions of mankind had their seats of empire in America," he announced. "Many of the mounds are completely occupied with human skeletons, and millions of them must have been interred in these vast cemeteries, that can be traced from the Rocky Mountains, on the west, to the Alleghenies on the east, and into the province of the Texas and New Mexico on the south: revolutions like those known in the old world, may have taken place here, and armies, equal to those of Cyrus, of Alexander the Great, or of Tamerlane the powerful, might have flourished their trumpets, and marched to battle, over these extensive plains."

Priest argued that America was the land where Noah's Ark came to rest and suggested that at least some of the mounds had been built before the Deluge. Surveying the various themes of Mound Builder origins, he could not decide whether the mounds were the work of Polynesians, Egyptians, Greeks, Romans, Israelites, Scandinavians, Welsh, Scots, or Chinese, though he felt certain the Indians had not built them. Of course, he provided the usual description of the last days of the Mound Builders, "making a last struggle against the invasion of an overwhelming foe; where, it is likely, they were reduced by famine, and perished amid the yells of their enemies."

Such writers as Priest posed as serious scholars; but poets and novelists were also beginning to be attracted by the theme of the Mound Builders. England's Robert Southey wrote a long poem, "Madoc," in 1805, describing the mounds as the ruins of cities built by a band of Welshmen who had sailed to the New World in the twelfth century. The first American poet to write of the Mound Builders, it seemed, was Sarah J. Hale of New Hampshire, whose "The Genius of Oblivion," published in 1823, portrayed the Mound Builders as the descendants of a pair of young Phoenician lovers who had fled from a cruel and tyrannical king. A much more important New England poet, William Cullen Bryant, also fell under the spell of the mounds. He won his first fame with "Thanatopsis," a poem written when he was 18; its theme was death, and one of its passages spoke of millions of ancient warriors lying entombed in the American mounds.

In 1832 Bryant, already an established voice in American literature, traveled to Illinois to visit his two brothers. Riding on horseback over the prairies, he paused to meditate on the ancient mounds and embankments, and the result was "The Prairies," a long work that shows how stirred Bryant was by the popular fantasies of the mounds, the tales of bygone heroes and forgotten battles. He tells of looking upon the mounds and thinking of those buried in them. "A race, that long has passed away, built them," he declares, and thinks of the days when the "disciplined and populous" Mound Builders farmed their fields and heaped up soil into mounds, until the day when

> The red man came—
> The roaming hunter tribes, warlike and fierce,
> And the mound-builders vanished from the earth.
> The solitude of centuries untold
> Has settled where they dwelt. The prairie-wolf
> Hunts in their meadows, and his fresh-dug den
> Yawns by my path. The gopher mines the ground
> Where stood the swarming cities. All is gone;
> All—save the piles of earth that hold their bones,
> The platforms where they worshipped unknown gods,
> The barriers which they builded from the soil
> To keep the foe at bay. . . .

Among the many novels dealing with the Mound Builders, a typical example is Cornelius Mathews' *Behemoth: A Legend of the Mound-Builders* (1839). Mathews pictures the continent thick with the great cities of civilized Mound Builders. A generation before he wrote, paleontologists had shown that giant bones frequently unearthed in America belonged to certain extinct elephant-like creatures known as mammoths and mastodons. Mathews invented a colossal mammoth named Behemoth, which terrorizes the Mound Builders by rampaging through their cities. The fortifications of earth they erect do not halt his charge; but finally a Mound Builder hero named Bokulla devises a way of penning the monster in, and kills it.

There were dozens of similar works. As late as 1864, Daniel Pierce Thompson enjoyed great success with his story, "Centeola; or, The Maid of the Mounds," which told of the sufferings of a lovely Mound Builder maiden and her lover. The two are about to meet a terrible death when a great earthquake saves them, though it destroys the Mound Builder civilization.

One imaginative young man who was fond of reading and theorizing about the Mound Builders was a farm boy named Joseph Smith, born in Vermont in 1805. "During our evening conversations," Smith's mother wrote many years later, "Joseph would occasionally give us some of the most amusing recitals that could be imagined. He would describe the ancient inhabitants of this continent, their dress, mode of traveling, and the animals upon which they rode; their cities, their buildings, with every particular; their mode of warfare; and also their religious worship. This he would do with as much ease, seemingly, as if he had spent his whole life with them." What is important about Joseph Smith's fascination with the Mound Builders is that it led him to found a religious movement that is still very active in the United States: the Church of Jesus Christ of Latter-day Saints, popularly known as the Mormon Church.

The subject of the origin of the Mormons is a delicate one. Those who accept the religion regard Joseph Smith as a divinely inspired prophet who ranks with Moses, Jesus, and Mohammed; those who scorn it look upon Smith as a fraud and upon his writings as long-winded fantasies. For every event in Mormon history there are two versions, one favorable to Smith, one bitterly hostile.

According to Smith's own account, he was unable to join any existing religious group as he grew up near Palmyra, New York, because none seemed satisfactory to him. In 1820, when he was fifteen, he experienced a mystic vision in which Jesus came to him and warned him to reject all religions of that day. Three years later he had another vision, in which a supernatural figure robed in white entered his bedroom and identified himself to Smith as the angel Moroni, a messenger of God. Smith said Moroni told him "that God had a work for me to do. . . . He said there was a book deposited, written upon gold plates, giving an account of the former inhabitants of this continent, and the source from whence they sprang. He also said that the fulness of the everlasting Gospel was contained in it; as delivered by the Savior to the ancient inhabitants." Smith was instructed to find the golden plates, translate the text they bore into English, and bring word of them to his fellow men.

Under Moroni's guidance, Smith went to a hill now called Cumorah, near Palmyra, and found the plates in a stone vault under a flat rock on the side of the hill. With them were two magical stones that Moroni said would allow Smith to do the translation. When he tried to take the plates out, however, Moroni told him the time had not yet come. Not until 1827 was Smith permitted to take the plates from the hill to begin his translation.

At once persecutions came upon him. His claim of

divine inspiration was met with scorn, and several times he was shot at or attacked by mobs. Realizing his danger, Joseph hid the plates in a barrel of beans and set out for his wife's family's farm in Pennsylvania. There, amid many difficulties, he and several disciples translated the plates, and in 1830 a printer in Palmyra produced 5,000 copies of the 588-page *Book of Mormon.* Afterward Moroni supposedly took back the plates, and no mortal ever saw them again; whether anyone but Smith has ever seen them is open to some doubt.

Now began the perilous growth of the Church of Latter-day Saints. Slowly Smith gathered followers, opposed at all times by bloody-minded mobs eager to stamp out the strange new religion. The Mormons were forced to flee into the West; Joseph Smith was lynched in an Illinois jail in 1844, and his followers continued to undergo severe persecution until, after an unsuccessful attempt to found a colony in Missouri, they trekked through the desert into unknown Utah. There they remain, no longer persecuted, but still controversial.

The *Book of Mormon,* which the Latter-day Saints consider as holy as the Old and New Testaments, is written in the style of the King James Bible, and deals mainly with battles and migrations. It opens with the account of Nephi of Jerusalem who, according to Smith, lived in the sixth century B.C.

Nephi describes how, long before his own day, at the time of the Confusion of Tongues following the building of the Tower of Babel, the Lord sent settlers from the Near East across the ocean to America. These were the Jaredites, named for Jared, their leader. In the New World they built great cities and reached a population of millions; but then civil war divided them, and they killed one another to the last man, with the final battle taking place near the hill Cumorah. Their homes become mere "heaps of earth upon the face of the land." But a Jaredite historian, Ether, survived long enough to set down on golden plates the account of his people's downfall. Ether predicts that in days to come new settlers will come to America and found a New Jerusalem.

Many centuries pass. About 600 B.C., in the time of Jeremiah, some Jews escape from the original Jerusalem just before its destruction by the Babylonians. They are led by Lehi, Nephi's father. With God's aid they survive their wanderings in the desert, learn how to build ships, cross the Atlantic, and settle in America, "choice among all other lands." As the vanished Jaredites had done before them, they prosper and multiply, build mighty cities, and surround them with huge fortifications. They find the golden plates inscribed by Ether, and learn of the history of the Jaredites.

But the cycle repeats itself. This second band of colonists splits into two factions, the Nephites and the Lamanites. The Nephites are rich, civilized agricultural people. But the Lamanites are ungodly savages and to punish them, God turns their skin a dark reddish hue. They are, in fact, the ancestors of the American Indians.

The Nephites grow corrupt and begin to worship idols. About A.D. 300, angered by the sins of the Nephites (who are the Mound Builders), God resolves to destroy their civilization. Their cities are invaded and laid waste by the Lamanites. Once more there is a great battle at the hill Cumorah, in A.D. 401; nearly all of the Nephites perish. Again, one priest-scholar survives to compose the history of his kind. This last Nephite is Mormon, who inscribes the record on golden plates (and includes a shorter version of Ether's earlier narrative). He gives the plates to his son Moroni, who in A.D. 421 deposits them in the stone vault on Cumorah. There they remain until discovered by Joseph Smith.

By some two million Americans today the *Book of Mormon* is considered at least as reliable a work of history as the Gospels or the Five Books of Moses. They believe it to be true that America was twice populated by emigrants from the Near East, that the mounds and embankments discovered by later European explorers are the cemeteries and fortifications of these vanished peoples, and that the Indians are descendants of ancient Israelites. But to those hostile to Mormonism, the sacred *Book of Mormon* is just another literary expression of the Mound Builder mythology.

Opponents of the Mormons have argued for more than a century that Joseph Smith was merely an overimaginative youth who became carried away by the fiction of the Mound Builders, and that he may have lifted much of the *Book of Mormon* from one or more books or unpublished manuscripts of Mound Builder fables that he happened to come across. Both sides in the dispute have advanced enormous quantities of evidence to back their charges and claims, and the truth is very much in doubt. What is certain, though, is that Joseph Smith was fascinated by the story of the Mound Builders and that he succeeded in founding a major religious creed whose scriptures offer an explanation of how the mounds came into being. The essence of the Mormon beliefs concerning the mounds can be summed up in the words of Orson Pratt, an early Mormon leader, who wrote in 1851:

"The bold, bad Lamanites, originally white, became dark and dirty. . . . They became wild, savage, and ferocious, seeking by every means the destruction of the prosperous Nephites, against whom they many times arrayed their hosts in battle. . . . The slain, frequently amounting to tens of thousands, were piled together in great heaps and over-spread with a thin covering of earth, which will satisfactorily account for those ancient mounds filled with human bones, so numerous at the present day, both in North and South America."

▲▲▲ 4

THE GREAT DEBATE

▲▲▲

By 1840, the country between the Alleghenies and the Mississippi was no longer a sparsely populated wilderness. The pioneer villages were becoming towns, and even cities; territories were achieving statehood; the once-troublesome Indian marauders had largely been pushed westward, beyond the rim of civilization. In Ohio and neighboring states, men now had time to take stock, to think and examine and study. In 1800, an Ohioan with a mound on his property was likely to level it so he could plant crops; forty years later it was more probable that he would undertake a careful excavation and fill his house with a collection of ancient artifacts. The feverish and romantic public interest in the Mound Builders led to a great deal of this amateur archaeologizing in the mound country and sparked a renewal of the debate on the origin of the mounds.

There was no shortage of imaginative philosophers trying to prove that the Mound Builders had been Israelites, Phoenicians, Malays, Irishmen, or members of some other immigrant group. But now, also, there were many out in the open country, soiling their hands in the earth of the mounds, men who split the tumuli apart and sought to base their judgments on some sort of solid evidence.

74

5   The Great Mound at Grave Creek. Engraving from
Ancient Monuments of the Mississippi Valley, by E. G.
Squier and E. H. Davis, 1848.

One of the important mound excavations of the day was
carried out in 1838 at the Grave Creek Mound on the
banks of the Ohio in what was then Virginia, but since 1863
has been West Virginia. This mound was one of the first
major earthworks to be discovered by white men and got
considerable attention in the late eighteenth century. A
report quoted in Caleb Atwater's paper on the mounds declares that in 1819 the mound was "one of the most august
monuments of remote Antiquity any where to be found. Its
circumference at the base, is 300 yards; its diameter, of
course, 100. Its altitude, from measurement, is 90 feet; and
its diameter, at the summit, is 45 feet. The centre, at the
summit, appears to have sunk several feet, so as to form a
small kind of amphitheatre. The rim enclosing this amphi-

theatre, is seven or eight feet in thickness. . . . This lofty and venerable tumulus has been so far opened, as to ascertain that it contains many thousands of human skeletons, but no farther. The proprietor of the ground, Mr. Joseph Tomlinson, will not suffer its demolition in the smallest degree. I, for one, do him honour for his sacred regard for these works of Antiquity. . . ."

On March 19, 1838, Abelard B. Tomlinson, a member of the family that owned the Grave Creek property, began to excavate the big mound. At a cost of $2,500, he sank a shaft from the "amphitheatre" at the summit of the mound to its base. At a depth of 77 feet he found a stone-covered, log-walled chamber enclosing a skeleton decorated with thousands of shell beads, copper rings, and mica plates. Going deeper, Tomlinson found another log-walled chamber 111 feet below the summit, in a pit that must have been dug before the mound was built. It contained two skeletons, one of them surrounded by 650 shell beads. A horizontal trench cut through the mound revealed masses of charcoal and burned bones, and ten more skeletons.

To modern archaeologists, Abelard Tomlinson's report on the Grave Creek dig is important because it provides the first clear description of the log tombs of what now is called the Adena Culture. Tomlinson's contemporaries, though, simply described the vaults as the tombs of Mound Builder kings, and turned their attention to a much more exciting discovery: the Grave Creek Tablet.

Tomlinson had found it in the mound in June, 1838. It was an oval white sandstone disc, ¾ of an inch thick and 1½ inches in diameter, on which were inscribed three lines in an unknown alphabet. The Mormon controversy was then raging; the whole nation knew of Joseph Smith and the golden plates he claimed to have found in the hill Cumorah. The uproar over the Grave Creek Tablet is easy to imagine.

Among those who came to Grave Creek to examine the tablet was Henry Rowe Schoolcraft (1793–1864), one of the great early figures in American anthropology. Trained as a geologist, Schoolcraft had become interested in Indians while exploring the country west of the Alleghenies; he had become an expert on Indian languages and folklore, and had even married a half-Indian girl. When he headed for Grave Creek in 1842, he was considered one of the nation's leading authorities on the native peoples of the Americas.

Schoolcraft pondered the 25 characters on the Grave Creek Tablet and decided that at least four of the letters bore strong resemblance to letters of the ancient Celtic alphabet of the British Isles. But he was not an expert on ancient Celtic, so he sent copies of the inscription to several European scholars. One claimed to see a kinship with the Libyan writing of North Africa; another ascribed the tablet to the Numidians, also of North Africa.

Opinions multiplied astonishingly as the controversy over the tablet drew in more experts. One man saw four characters he claimed were ancient Greek; another saw ten Phoenician letters; another, fourteen old British letters; and so on. Then came attempts at translation, though no one yet agreed what kind of writing was on the tablet. In 1857, Maurice Schwab of France published his version: "The Chief of Emigration who reached these places (or this island) has fixed these statutes forever." A decade later Jules Oppert, who played a key part in deciphering the cuneiform writing of the Sumerians of Mesopotamia, pro-

vided a different interpretation of the Grave Creek mes-
sage: "The grave of one who was assassinated here. May
God to avenge him strike his murderer, cutting off the hand
of his existence." And in 1873 M. Levy Bing told a meeting
of anthropologists in France that he had found 23 Canaanite letters on the tablet which said, "What thou sayest, thou
dost impose it, thou shinest in thy impetuous clan and rapid
chamois." This nonsensical version inspired little confidence,
and thereafter there were few serious attempts to "translate"
the Grave Creek Tablet.

Schoolcraft published an account of his Grave Creek
researches and his general thoughts on the Mound Builders
in 1845. At that time he seemed to believe that the Mound
Builders had been a race distinct from and superior to the
Indians, although he did not put this idea forward very
strongly. Among the evidence he offered were several skillfully cut stone tubes, eight to twelve inches long and about
an inch wide, that had been found in one mound; he thought
that these elegantly carved relics might be some kind of
"telescopic tubes," indicating that the Mound Builders had
been practicing astronomers. But he proposed this only as
an extremely tentative guess, and he soon backed away from
the idea. His final views on the mounds appeared in his
huge six-volume work, *The Indian Tribes of the United
States,* which was published between 1851 and 1857.

In the first volume of this vast enterprise Schoolcraft expressed the opinion that the mounds were the work of the
ancestors of the North American Indians, and not of a fan-
cied nation of Mound Builders. He commented: "There
is little to sustain a belief that these ancient works are due
to tribes of more fixed and exalted traits of civilization, far

less to a people of an expatriated type of civilization, of either an ASIATIC or EUROPEAN origin, as several popular writers very vaguely, and with little severity of investigation, imagined. . . . There is nothing, indeed, in the magnitude and structure of our western mounds which a semi-hunter and semi-agricultural population, like that which may be ascribed to the ancestors of Indian predecessors of the existing race, could not have executed." He criticized the "spirit of misapprehension and predisposition to exaggeration" of many of his archaeological colleagues.

This was a forthright and uncompromising statement, and, in terms of its era, an astonishing one; it was the first time in nearly thirty years that anyone of note had said such things. Schoolcraft was ahead of his time by at least a generation, and his views were ignored by those convinced of the truth of the Mound Builder fantasy.

2

While Abelard Tomlinson was sinking his shaft at Grave Creek, a distinguished American physician was seeking the answer to the mound riddle in another way. He was Dr. Samuel G. Morton of Philadelphia, who has been termed the father of American physical anthropology.

Born in 1799, Morton began to practice medicine in 1826, and carried out special research in anatomy, attempting particularly to determine how the various races of mankind differed in body structure. He developed methods for analyzing a skull to discover its owner's race; between 1830 and the year of his death, 1851, Morton assembled 968 skulls, the largest collection of its kind then in existence.

Included in his gallery of skulls were a number that came
from mounds and Indian sites, and Morton applied his
measuring techniques in an effort to discover if the Mound
Builders and the Indians were indeed separate races.

He was not the first to have made such studies. In 1819,
Caleb Atwater had examined skeletons in Ohio burial
mounds, concluding that they "never belonged to a people
like our Indians. The latter are a tall, rather slender,
straight limbed people; the former [the Mound Builders]
were short and thick." Ten years later, Dr. McCulloh of
Baltimore examined some mound burials and came to just
the opposite conclusion: that the Mound Builders and the
Indians were physically of the same race.

Using instruments he had invented himself, Morton
measured hundreds of skulls, taking ten measurements on
each. In 1839, he published his findings in an impressive
volume called *Crania Americana,* handsomely illustrated
with drawings of his specimens. Eight of the skulls he had
studied had come from mounds. Three had been found in
burial mounds in Peru; one was from the Grave Creek
Mound, one from a mound near Circleville, Ohio, and the
other three came from Tennessee, Alabama, and Wisconsin.
He compared these with each other and with the skulls of
four recent Indians of Ohio and two skulls from Mammoth
Cave, Kentucky. Morton's table of measurements showed
that there was no significant difference between the eight
Mound Builder skulls, the four modern Indian skulls from
Ohio, and the two from Mammoth Cave, although American natives as a whole appeared to belong to a race distinct
from those in other parts of the world. He concluded "that
the American nations, excepting the Polar tribes [the

Eskimos] were of one Race and one Species. . . ."

Having lumped Mound Builders and Indians into a single race, Morton nevertheless felt he had to account for the cultural gap separating the high civilizations of Mexico from the simple nomadic Indians of the United States. Thus he divided his American Indian race into two families, the "Toltecan" and the "Barbarous." The various Mexican civilizations he assigned to the Toltecan group; he felt that the Mound Builders, too, were probably Toltecan. All other American tribes were put in the Barbarous family, whose members had "decidedly inferior" intellectual abilities.

Despite these dubious conclusions, Morton had made a valuable contribution by demonstrating the racial unity of the American Indians and their mound-building predecessors. But those who still insisted that there had been a non-Indian race of Mound Builders complained that conclusions based on the study of a mere five skulls from the North American mounds need not be accepted as final. Some argued that Morton had mistaken modern skulls buried in old mounds for authentic relics of Mound Builders. So, despite the care and labor that went into Morton's researches, the case against Mound Builders as a separate race remained unproven. It was possibly just as well that it did, for later anthropologists showed that Morton had reached the right conclusion using faulty, incomplete, and erroneous data. Mound Builders and American Indians did indeed both belong to the same racial stock; but that did not at all mean that they were identical in appearance. These subtleties, though, were decades away from being understood when Samuel Morton died, twelve years after the publication of *Crania Americana*.

3

It was time once more for a major study of the mounds.
A quarter of a century had passed since Caleb Atwater's
pioneering essay. Atwater had scarcely dealt with mounds
outside Ohio, while his hasty surveys of the Ohio mounds
had not been of scholarly quality. And his theories concerning the mounds, good enough in 1820, seemed naïve
and inadequate by 1845. The American Ethnological Society, led by Gallatin and Schoolcraft, began a search for a
man who would compile all that was known about the
mounds, conduct extensive new research, and produce a
definitive study.

The man they found for the job was Ephraim George
Squier (1821–1888), a newspaper editor and part-time
politician. Squier, born in New York, had settled in Chillicothe, Ohio, in 1844. Chillicothe is situated in the very
heart of the Ohio mound country, and soon Squier was
spending whatever time his newspaper did not require in
examining the prehistoric earthworks in his vicinity. In
company with Dr. E. H. Davis, a Chillicothe physician,
Squier opened over two hundred mounds, explored about a
hundred earthen enclosures, and gathered a sizable collection of artifacts, all between 1845 and 1847. In addition
the two men surveyed many of the earthworks quite ex-
pertly, preparing detailed contour maps of acceptable accuracy and, incidentally, of great beauty.

During this time they received encouragement and finan-
cial support from the American Ethnological Society. In
1846, Squier appeared before that group to discuss his
work. He said, "At the outset all preconceived notions were

abandoned, and the work of research commenced, as if no speculations had been indulged in, nor anything before been known, respecting the singular remains of antiquity scattered so profusely around us." There have been "too few well-authenticated facts," he declared, and "their absence has been purely supplied by speculations."

Shortly Squier announced that he was nearing completion of a book that would run to some 300 large and lavishly illustrated pages when published. The American Ethnological Society, only five years old, did not have the funds to pay for publication of such a work; and so aid was sought from an even younger but much wealthier body, the Smithsonian Institution.

James Smithson, a rich and eccentric Englishman, had left his fortune to the United States to found "an establishment for the increase and diffusion of knowledge among men." No one knew why Smithson had given his money to the United States, which he had never even visited, but after some debate the gift was accepted and the Smithsonian Institution came into being on August 10, 1846. The physicist Joseph Henry became its first head.

Henry planned to publish a series of large scientific volumes called *Smithsonian Contributions to Knowledge.* Hardly had he assumed his position as secretary of the Institution when the officers of the American Ethnological Society came to him with Squier's massive mound manuscript. Henry was not interested in mounds, but he wanted to begin his series of books; and so it happened that the first volume in the series was the majestic *Ancient Monuments of the Mississippi Valley,* bearing the by-line of E. G. Squier, A.M., and E. H. Davis, M.D.

So began the involvement of the Smithsonian Institution

with the Mound Builders. The second, third, seventh, and eighth volumes of *Smithsonian Contributions to Knowledge* would also contain essays on the mounds, while in the next generation one branch of the Smithsonian would launch the most intensive study of the mounds ever undertaken.

Ancient Monuments of the Mississippi Valley, when it came off the press in 1848, instantly established itself as a work of commanding importance in American archaeology. As a summary of knowledge in its particular field at that time, it was remarkable; as a model for later work, it was invaluable; as a detailed record of the Ohio mounds as they appeared in 1847, it was and still is unique.

In his opening pages, Squier—for he did most of the writing, despite the shared by-line—reviews the work of his predecessors, mentioning William Bartram, Bishop Madison, the Reverend Mr. Harris, DeWitt Clinton, and many others back to de Soto. He gives Atwater credit for "the first attempt towards a general account of the ancient monuments of the West," though noting that his paper "contains many errors, for which however we can find a ready apology in the unsettled state of the country, and the attendant difficulties . . . at the time it was written, —errors which, under present advantages of research, would be inexcusable." He states his own intention of abandoning preconceived notions and theories, and this he observes fairly faithfully throughout his report.

After some preliminary words on the geographic distribution of the ancient earthworks, Squier classifies them by types, dividing them into two groups: mounds and enclosures, the latter taking in all walls and embankments. Then he subclassifies mounds as burial mounds, temple mounds, mounds of sacrifice, and so forth.

In his discussion of enclosures Squier argues that most of the lowland earthworks were probably religious centers, since they could not have served any effective defensive purpose. As for the hilltop embankments, he writes: "The natural strength of such positions . . . would certainly suggest them as the citadels of a people having hostile neighbors, or pressed by invaders. . . . While rugged and steep on most sides, they have one or more points of comparatively easy approach, in the protection of which the utmost skill of the builders seems to have been exhausted. They are guarded by double, overlapping walls, or a series of them, having sometimes an accompanying mound, designed perhaps for a look-out. . . ."

Squier presents a series of descriptions of individual forts, based on his and Davis's personal examinations. Each is accompanied by a detailed map, drawn by Squier from survey work done in some cases by himself and Davis, in some cases by others. Squier's draftsmanship is elegant and the plans are delightful to behold. Today visitors to some of the surviving Ohio earthworks can see blown-up photos of charts from Squier and Davis on display as a guide to the monuments.

Some of the ancient fortifications Squier discusses still exist, such as Fort Hill, in Highland County, Ohio, and Fort Ancient, in Warren County, Ohio. But most have long since disappeared. By counting the rings in the trunk of a large chestnut tree atop Fort Hill, Squier concluded that the fort was at least a thousand years old. He regarded this fort and others like it as excellently designed, and he had a high opinion of "the judgment, skill, and industry of their builders." He wrote that no one can examine the forts without feeling "the conviction that the race, by whom these works

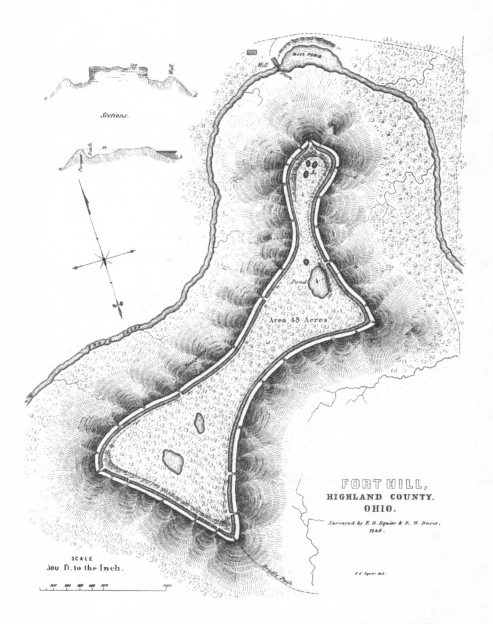

FORT HILL,
HIGHLAND COUNTY,
OHIO.

Surveyed by E. G. Squier & E. H. Davis,
1846.

Sections.

Area 48 Acres

SCALE
500 ft. to the Inch.

6   Diagram of the Fort Hill works. Squier and Davis, 1848.

were erected, possessed no inconsiderable knowledge of the science of defence,—a degree of knowledge much superior to that known to have been possessed by the hunter tribes of North America previous to the discovery by Columbus, or indeed subsequent to that event." Thus Squier joined the ranks of believers in the fabled Mound Builders.

As had Caleb Atwater, Squier seemed to think that the Mound Builders' civilization "spread southward, constantly developing itself in its progress, until it attained its height in Mexico." The presence of the forts led him to think that the migration was not voluntary. He traces a diagonal line of fortifications across the continent from western New York State through central and northern Ohio into southern Illinois, and from this he infers that out of the northeast "came the hostile savage hordes, before whose incessant attacks the less warlike mound-builders gradually receded, or beneath whose exterminating cruelty those who occupied this frontier entirely disappeared, leaving these monuments alone to attest their existence, and the extraordinary skill with which they defended their altars and their homes. . . . It is clear that the contest was a protracted one, and that the race of the mounds were for a long period constantly exposed to attack."

The second part of Squier's book is devoted to what he called "sacred enclosures." It seemed to him, as it also has seemed to most modern observers, that the geometrical earthworks of the Ohio Valley must have been religious in purpose. He speaks of the "devotional fervor or superstitious zeal which induced their erection," and expresses awe at their size: "It is difficult to comprehend the existence of religious works, extending . . . like those near Newark [Ohio] over an area of little less than *four square miles!*"

With many attractive diagrams he proceeds to describe
the enclosures and walled avenues of southern Ohio: the
Mound City group north of Chillicothe; the ancient works
at Liberty Township and on Paint Creek; Ross County's
High Bank, Hopeton, and Cedar Bank earthworks; those of
Seal Township, Pike County; and in particular the imposing
octagon and circle of Newark. Most of these are gone today.

Not only the size but also the precision of the enclosures
awes Squier. *"The Builders,"* he says, and the italics are his,
*"possessed a standard of measurement, and had some means
of determining angles.* The most skilful engineer of the day
would find it difficult, without the aid of instruments, to lay
down an accurate square of the great dimensions of those
above represented, measuring as they do more than *four
fifths* of a mile in circumference. It would not, it is true, be
impossible to construct circles of considerable size, without
instruments; the difficulty of doing so, when we come to the
construction of works five thousand four hundred feet, or
over a mile in circumference, is nevertheless apparent. But
we not only find accurate squares and perfect circles, but
also, as we have seen, *octagons* of great dimensions." Although it was the mere bulk of burial mounds such as that
at Grave Creek, and temple mounds such as Cahokia, that
had fascinated earlier observers, the intricate structure of
the Ohio enclosures was now becoming the most mystify-
ing aspect of the story, and the one most likely to keep
alive the concept of a superior race.

Turning to the Southern mounds, Squier confesses: "We
are in possession of very little authentic information respecting the monuments of the Southern United States." Unlike
Ohioans, Southerners had displayed remarkably little curiosity about the mounds in their midst. No one since William

Bartram's day, seventy years before, had attempted a detailed exploration of the Southern mounds, and Squier had to rely on the sketchy reports of men who had examined one or two earthworks apiece.

It had been clear since the eighteenth century that the huge, flat-topped Southern mounds were basically different in type from the conical, rounded burial mounds of the Ohio Valley. Though some conical mounds were found in the Southern states, Squier notes, they are "overshadowed by the more remarkable structures which surrounded them." The lack of any report of a mound excavation in the South made it difficult for Squier to say much about the origin and purpose of these big mounds. River erosion and landslides had revealed that some of them were made up of alternating platforms of earth and clay; others consisted of layers of earth and sand, or even of earth and human bones. Within them, apparently, were deposits of human remains, tools, pottery, and ornaments, often revealing great artistic skill. "It is impossible, with our present limited knowledge concerning them," Squier writes, "to form anything like a determinate or satisfactory conclusion respecting the numerous and remarkable remains of the South. The immense mounds that abound there may be vast sepulchres in which the remains of generations were deposited; they may have been the temples and 'high places' of a superstitious people, where rites were celebrated and sacrifices performed; or, they may have answered as the places of last resort, where, when pursued by foes, the ancient people fled to receive the support of their gods and to defend the altars of their religion."

Squier is equally uncertain who built the Southern mounds. Perhaps they were the work of a people contemporary with, but different from, the Ohio Mound Builders. Or possibly they were built by the Ohio people in the course of a migration southward. But he also suggests that the Ohio mounds may represent the work of colonists expanding northward from Mississippi and Florida, or even from Mexico or Peru.

Leaving the puzzles of the South, Squier turns to the mysteries of the Northwest, which then consisted of Wisconsin, Michigan, and Minnesota. This was the land of the effigy mounds. These low hummocks of earth or clay, modeled in the forms of animals, men, or abstract figures, had first been written about by one Richard C. Taylor in 1838, but no one before Squier had given a comprehensive survey of them. Squier reproduces many of the outline plans drawn by Taylor and others, with suggestions that they represent otter, buffalo, lizards, turtles, bears, and many other creatures. He is not sure whether they were done by outlying settlements of Ohio Mound Builders or if they were produced by an entirely separate culture, but "certain it is that they are now invaded by a busy population, careless alike of their origin and of their future fate, before whose encroachments they are rapidly disappearing."

At the halfway point in his book, Squier reaches the monuments he knows best: Ohio's burial mounds. "Within these mounds," he says, "we must look for the only authentic remains of their builders. They are the principal depositories of ancient art; they cover the bones of the distinguished dead of remote ages; and hide from the profane gaze of invading races the altars of the ancient people."

He divides the mounds into several categories. His class of Altar Mounds, he says, occurs only near "enclosures or sacred places." They contain "symmetrical altars of burned

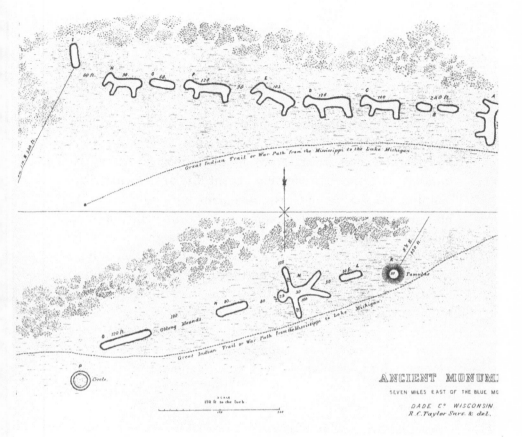

7   Diagram of Wisconsin effigy mounds. Squier and Davis, 1848.

clay or stone; on which are deposited various remains, which in all cases have been more or less subjected to the action of fire." Typical of this class, he notes, is the Mound City group, which, in 1847, was a collection of 26 mounds within one enclosure, on the banks of the Scioto River three miles north of Chillicothe, Ohio. Squier and Davis had excavated many of these mounds by driving shafts through them from their summits, and the report Squier gives shows that he and his colleague were careful and painstaking archaeologists, keeping track of the various materials making up each mound and the levels in which the main artifacts were found.

Squier knew that some of the things found in mounds had been put there long after the mounds were built. Thus he identified certain skeletons in the upper levels of the mounds as those of relatively recent Indians; local tribes simply used the mounds as convenient burying places. He also notes that "modern implements and ornaments, in some cases of European origin, are found with the recent burials. The necessity, therefore, of a careful and rigid discrimination, between these deposits and those of the mound-builders, will be apparent. From the lack of such discrimination, much misapprehension and confusion have resulted. Silver crosses, gun-barrels, and French dial-plates, have been found with skeletons in the mounds; yet it is not to be concluded that the mound-builders were Catholics, or used firearms, or understood French. . . . It may be safely assumed, that whatever deposits occur near the surface of the mounds, are of a date subsequent to their erection."

After discussing several other categories of mounds, including burial mounds and temple mounds, Squier proceeds to his most original contribution, a lengthy analysis of the styles of art found in the mounds. No one had attempted such a survey before; and though Squier was wrong in many details, he provided a point of departure for his successors.

He begins with pottery—"the first domestic art practiced by man." Squier was familiar with many types of Indian pottery, from the crude ware of the North to the more sophisticated products of the Gulf Coast and the masterpieces of Mexico and Peru. Very little pottery had then been found in the Ohio mounds, and almost none in those of the South, but Squier asserts, "Among the mound-builders the art of pottery attained to a considerable degree of perfection. Various though not abundant specimens of their skill have been recovered which, in elegance of model, delicacy, and finish, as also in fineness of material, come fully up to the best Peruvian specimens, to which they bear, in many respects, a close resemblance." In terms of the mound pottery known in 1847, this was much too generous, and even the extraordinary Arkansas and Tennessee pots unearthed a generation later fall well short of the standards of Peru, although they have a certain beauty of their own. But the high rating Squier gives to Mound Builder pottery is part of his underlying theory; he insists that their pots "far exceed anything of which the existing tribes of Indians are known to have been capable," and the theme recurs as he takes up other types of artifacts.

In discussing the metal implements from the mounds, he points out that the Mound Builders apparently made use only of copper and silver, two metals that could be found pure in nature and hammered into shape. He doubts that they were able to smelt metals from ores or to use such advanced techniques as casting to manufacture metal goods. He writes: "No iron or traces of iron, except with the recent deposits, have been discovered; nor is it believed that the race of the mounds had any knowledge of that metal."

With many fine woodcuts Squier depicts the copper axes, bracelets, and spear points from the mounds; he shows finely wrought weapon points of chipped stone, some so delicate that they must have been purely ornamental pieces; he illustrates grooved axes of stone, and celts, or polished grooveless hand axes. He shows the odd, attractive stone implements called bannerstones, which he believes might have been the heads of ceremonial hatchets. (No one knows even yet what they were used for, though many authorities think they served as weights for *atlatls,* or spear-throwing devices.) He portrays awls and needles of bone, and the curious stone objects known as discoidals, which were probably pieces in a prehistoric game. He shows the stone pipes from the mounds, and he speaks of Mound Builder beads of shell and the fresh-water pearls that bedazzled de Soto's men. He describes "gorgets," flat pendant ornaments worn on necklaces, and shows the strange abstract "birdstones" found in many sites.

In addition to these everyday objects Squier discusses "a large class of remains, comprising sculptural tablets, and heads and figures of animals, which belongs to a higher grade of art. Many of these exhibit a close observance of nature and a minute attention to details, such as we could only expect to find among a people considerably advanced in the minor arts. . . ." Referring to American Indian art as the "clumsy and ungraceful" production of savages, Squier attempts to prove from the supposed superiority of Mound Builder art that the Mound Builders must have been a race different from and far more civilized than the Indians. But later archaeologists found Squier's arguments unconvincing.

He spends little time on the inscribed tablets from the mounds, with their supposed alphabetic and hieroglyphic messages. Noting that not even the great Mexican civilizations had arrived at the use of writing, he points out that it would be unwise to credit the Mound Builders, who were less advanced, with such a skill. Most of the tablets, besides, are probably fakes, Squier remarks. He mentions six inscribed brass plates four inches long that had turned up in 1843 in a mound near Kinderhook, Illinois. They bore "ancient characters," said to resemble Chinese. With the nation in an uproar over the Mormons, the discovery of the plates won wide attention, but, Squier tells, "subsequent inquiry has shown that the plates were a harmless imposition, got up for local effect." The village blacksmith, taking his inspiration for the hieroglyphics from the lettering on the lid of a Chinese tea chest, had produced them.

A tablet that Squier does not dismiss, and which archaeologists still consider authentic, is the Cincinnati Tablet, a sandstone slab five inches long and about three inches wide that was found in a mound in 1841. Pondering the strange pattern of curves engraved on the tablet's face, Squier rejects several mystic interpretations of its meaning and proposes tentatively that the tablet was a stamp used for imprinting ornaments on the clothes or the skins of its makers.

His "Concluding Observations" are brief and clearly stated. He expresses his belief in a widespread civilization of Mound Builders maintaining essentially the same customs, habits, religion, and government throughout the Ohio Valley. The size and scope of such earthworks as the Newark embankments and the Cahokia Mound prove, for Squier, that the ancient population must have been extremely large, for, working with simple stone and wooden tools, thousands of men must have been employed in these projects. So dense a population could have been supported only by an agricultural economy. He does not attempt to explain why the Mound Builders disappeared, or where they might have gone. Many mysteries remain, he says,

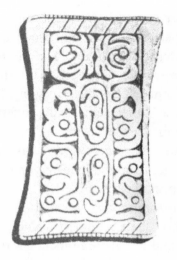

8   The Cincinnati tablet. Engraving from *Ancient Monuments of the Mississippi Valley,* by E. G. Squier and E. H. Davis, 1848.

ending with the statement, "Further and more extended investigations and observations may, nevertheless, serve satisfactorily to settle not only this, but other equally interesting questions connected with the extinct race, whose name is lost to tradition itself, and whose very existence is left to the sole and silent attestation of the rude but often imposing monuments which throng the valleys of the West."

5

The Whigs—the political party Squier supported—won the Presidential election in 1848, the year his *Ancient Monuments of the Mississippi Valley* came out. The Ohio newspaperman had become a national figure because of his book—it is hard for us to realize the impact that any sizable study of the Mound Builders had on Americans of the mid-nineteenth century—and the newly elected President, Zachary Taylor, was rewarding scientific zeal as well as political support when he named Squier to a diplomatic post in Central America. Squier hoped to learn more about the origin of the Mound Builders while he was south of the border. He did not succeed in this, but he did have a long and notable career there in diplomacy, in business, and in archaeology, making important investigations in Nicaragua and Peru. Before leaving the United States, though, he returned to his native state of New York for a survey of the mounds of its western counties. His report, published by the Smithsonian in 1849, presented the view that the New York earthworks, unlike those of Ohio, were fairly recent and had been built by the Iroquois or a neighboring Indian tribe.

Before he left, Squier also tried to sell his collection of Mound Builder relics. No purchaser would meet his price, however, and the artifacts remained in storage until 1864, when they were bought by William Blackmore of London. Blackmore wanted to donate them to some worthy American museum, but some museums (including the Smithsonian) were not interested in having them, and others did not have space to display them properly. Finally Blackmore took Squier's collection to England, where it eventually found a home in London's British Museum.

The Smithsonian continued to publish papers on the mounds. The third volume of the *Smithsonian Contributions to Knowledge* (1852) carried a paper by Charles Whittlesey, "Descriptions of Ancient Works in Ohio," and three years later the seventh volume offered an essay by Increase A. Lapham on the effigy mounds of Wisconsin. In 1856,

Samuel F. Haven, the librarian of the American Antiquarian Society, presented his views on the mounds in the eighth of the *Smithsonian Contributions*. His long article was entitled, "Archaeology of the United States, or Sketches Historical and Bibliographical, of the Progress of Information and Opinion Respecting Vestiges of Antiquity in the United States." It was not a report on original archaeological research, but an attempt at evaluating the work done by others on American prehistory up to that time.

Haven's approach is calm and wise. He condemns those writers who have been "seduced into idle speculation founded on superficial resemblances" in trying to establish one or another foreign people as the builders of the mounds, and suggests that they should have been "seeking the answer in the mounds themselves." Concerning the theories of Barton, Atwater, and Squier and Davis, Haven remarks that "none have led to a satisfactory solution."

His own notion of what a satisfactory solution would be is quite unromantic. He expresses the view that the allegedly civilized and superior Mound Builders were not really so advanced at all; comparing the Ohio and Mississippi Valley structures with those of Mexico, Central America, and Peru, he observes that in the United States mound regions "there are no ruins of temples or other structures of stone, wrought by the hammer or the chisel, such as abound in Central America. There are no traces of roads and bridges. . . . There are no proofs of the practice of reducing metals from their ores, and melting and casting them for use and ornament—none of a knowledge of chemistry or astronomy. . . . In a word, tokens of civil institutions, of mechanical employments, and the cultivation of science and literature however humbly such as appear among the remains of Mexico and Peruvian civilization, have no positive counterpart in the regions of which we are speaking. . . ." Much later, in the 1877 *Report of the American Antiquarian Society,* Haven was even more positive in expressing his belief that the Mound Builders had had no extraordinary civilization—that they and the "red Indians" were of the same race.

6

Perhaps Haven was too harsh on the mound folk, downgrading their abilities more than necessary in order to make up for the exaggerations of most other observers. But his cool, thoughtful assessment was preferable to the mythological nonsense that other writers were again pouring out on the American public. In the 1850's that public was rushing to buy a queer, jumbled book by William Pidgeon called *Traditions of De-coo-dah and Antiquarian Researches,* which offered wonderful and fantastic tales about the mounds.

Pidgeon claimed to be a trader with long experience among the Indians of the American West. He begins his book with a long pseudo-historical account of the mounds, crediting Adam with being the first builder of mounds, followed by Noah and his three sons, who carried the idea of mound-building to every continent. Pidgeon cites assorted evidence to "prove" that a variety of foreigners came to the United States before Columbus and built mounds. The earthworks at Marietta, Ohio, he says, were built by Romans; those of Wisconsin were fashioned by Danes, Bel-

gians, and Saxons; others were Phoenician, Hindu, or Afri-
can. Having established all this within six pages, Pidgeon
proceeds to drop it almost completely. For most of his book
he is concerned only with the fate of the Mound Builders
and their replacement by the Indians, rather than with their
origins in Europe, Asia, or Africa.

"It can not be any longer doubted," he says, "that there
has been a day when this continent swarmed with millions
of inhabitants, when the arts and sciences flourished, when
men lived, and labored, . . . and fought, and were in turn
conquerors and conquered, subjects and kings, where now
the deep silence of the forest has overcome all such evidences of life and civilization."

His interest in mounds, he relates, began in 1812 when
he was a young man in Virginia and came upon a cone-
shaped stone mound. An older friend told him that such
mounds were "dedicated to the great, containing only the
relics of great kings, prophets, and chiefs of signal renown,"
and Pidgeon and his schoolmates opened it, finding it full
of brittle, decaying bones. That kindled a desire to know
more about the mounds.

After some explorations in South America, Pidgeon set up
shop in 1829 as an Indian trader in Ohio's Miami Valley
and toured the mound country. His base of operations was
near Fort Ancient, the hilltop earthwork some 35 miles
northeast of Cincinnati, and his "thirst for investigation was
continually augmented by frequent conversations with antiquarians and curious travellers" who visited this "stupendous and wonderful" embankment.

In 1837, 1838, and 1839, business took him to the effigy-
mound country of Wisconsin. "Perceiving that those
mounds which were most remote from civilization retained

their primitive form in greatest perfection, I resolved to make a tour of exploration in the unfrequented wilds of the west; and, in the spring of 1840, I repaired to the city of St. Louis, whence I embarked on the steamer *Illinois* for Galena, in the early part of April."

Making his way northward by river, stopping off now and then to examine mounds along the way, Pidgeon finally came to the "somewhat dilapidated" old village of Prairie du Chien, Wisconsin. He stayed awhile among the friendly French trappers and half-breed Indians of this outpost, and through them came to know the Indians of the vicinity. He learned their language, attended some of their feasts, and visited them frequently.

Pidgeon's new Indian friends were displeased when he began to excavate the Wisconsin mounds. It developed that he was digging in "the graves of their departed friends," and they offered to guide him to other mounds just as interesting to him but not sacred to them. They took him to a "flat embankment 130 feet square, with an oval mound on the top, having an elevation of 14 feet, the flat embankment being two and a half feet high. On sinking a spade in the small mound, I discovered that it was composed of ashes, small particles of charcoal, and sand. . . ." Pidgeon rolled up his sleeves and began to dig, while his Indian companions sat by, grinning. Soon he came to the clay core of the mound. "But being much fatigued with my labor, I retired to the shade of a small tree which grew near by to rest myself; and while sitting there, wondering within myself what the anticipated relic would prove to be, an aged Winnebago squaw, whom curiosity had drawn to the spot, ascended the mound to view the excavation. She shook her blanket, and approached me; and, perceiving that I was fatigued, she presented to me a bladder filled with whiskey, and desired me to drink. I drank sparingly, and returned to my labor. She followed me to the pit, and looking into it, she thus addressed me—'Ah, how-she-mo-ko-mon, wah-wonk; cow-ean shu-rah; she-mo-ko-mon, sketch-ah-waw-wonk;' being interpreted, 'Ho, white man, you are a fool! There is no money there. White man, you are a very great fool!' and she went away, amid peals of laughter from the surrounding group."

The old squaw indeed had the last laugh, for the mound turned out to contain nothing of interest. But soon Pidgeon had more reliable guidance from "an aged Indian acquainted with the history of the mounds, whose name was De-coo-dah, a man of undoubted veracity, revered and respected by those that knew him." Pidgeon gained an introduction to De-coo-dah, and through an interpreter explained to the grim old man that he had come to survey and sketch the mounds, and wished to know their significance, so that coming generations might understand the history of the early occupants of the continent.

De-coo-dah spoke angrily of white men, who, he said, cared little for the mounds and destroyed them at whim or for their convenience. "Why does not the white man leave the record on the earth where it belongs?" But Pidgeon assured him that not all white men were so ignorant and selfish. De-coo-dah studied him for a minute and, turning to the interpreter, exclaimed, "A good man—a good white man!" Pidgeon goes on, "Again fixing on me his eyes that now beamed with benevolence, he added, 'The red man's friend,' and extended his hand. . . ." They smoked the pipe of friendship together, and all was well.

Through the winter of 1840–41, and again in 1841–42,

Pidgeon and the man he calls his "adopted father" lived together in a cabin on an island near Prairie du Chien. It was several months before De-coo-dah decided that Pidgeon could be trusted with his people's ancient traditions; but finally De-coo-dah began to speak of the past. He explained that he was not a member of any existing tribe, but was descended from "the Elk nation, now extinct," who were themselves descended from "those ancient Americans, the mound-builders."

Mound burial was a sacred Elk tradition. The making of effigy mounds was another. So too was the building of mounds to mark great national events. De-coo-dah, who

9 De-Coo-Dah. Engraving from *Traditions of De-Coo-Dah,* by William Pidgeon, 1858.

claimed to be in his 89th winter, said he had learned of
these things from his great-grandfather, who had died 78
years earlier at the age of 115. "My great-grandfather," De-
coo-dah told Pidgeon, "had a great reverence for mounds;
and said, that a new mound was erected at each national
festival; that national festivals were frequently attended and
held in union by several nations; and that at the place appointed for those union festivals, each nation erected a
national monument significant of their number and dignity."

The wild and fantastic story Pidgeon says De-coo-dah
told him asserts that the shape of a mound symbolizes the
events at the time of its construction. For instance, he
mentions the Amalgamation Mound on the Wisconsin River
about 50 miles above its junction with the Mississippi—a
group of effigies showing the outlines of two gigantic beasts
and a man. According to De-coo-dah, the horns of the
beasts stand for warriors: "One horn being longer than the
other, shows one nation to have been the stronger of the
two; and one horn having more prongs than the other,
represents one nation as having more celebrated chiefs than
the other. . . ." At another mound site, a group of small
mounds commemorates the marriages of seven chiefs during
the construction work, while three very small mounds near
one of the "matrimonial mounds" denote the birth of three
children.

Armed with the teachings of De-coo-dah, Pidgeon gives
his interpretations of the 400 earthworks he claims to have
visited in and around Wisconsin, as well as the more familiar ones of Ohio. Fort Ancient is the first to be discussed.
Pidgeon quickly disposes of the notion that this embankment could have been constructed "by the ancestors of the

present race of Indians. The natural indolence of the Indian and his averseness to any kind of manual labor are well known. But these works bear testimony to a degree of enterprise and of patient industry, that would bring no discredit to any race or nation known to history." Pidgeon rejects the obvious idea that Fort Ancient's purpose was defensive. From De-coo-dah he has learned that its real name is Moon City, and that its walls "were constructed by the successive labors of a long line of kings or rulers." Its purpose was religious, and its crescent shape indicates to him that it was a center for the worship of the Moon.

The huge Newark enclosures, says Pidgeon, were once "a prophet's metropolis, or holy seminary of priests or prophets, with its holy circles, festival square, secluded walks, private avenues, and funeral-piles. The five residential circles were the permanent abodes of the senior fathers, who were appointed by the people to impart instruction to the junior prophets. . . ." Near Chillicothe, De-coo-dah identified "the ruling prophet's resident circle," "the holy city," "the celestial city," and "the royal union city." When Pidgeon presented De-coo-dah with a diagram he had made of the Circleville earthwork, "his eyes beamed with delight, and he exclaimed, 'Sci-o-tee!' But when I informed him that a populous village now stood within the walls of the ancient enclosure, his frame trembled with emotion, and his visage grew dark with anger. I observed his excited state, and sought to change the subject. But my efforts were in vain, for memories of that ancient work seemed to engross all his thoughts. He soon, however, became more composed, and again repeated, as if to himself, 'Sci-o-tee!' . . . With an apparently unconscious movement of his hand toward the handle of his knife, he asked, 'Do the bones of my fathers rest in peace?' "

In warmer weather, so Pidgeon relates, he and De-coo-dah visited many of the effigy mounds of Wisconsin. At a "Sacrificial Pentagon" on the Kickapoo River 30 miles northeast of Prairie du Chien, De-coo-dah told Pidgeon of human sacrifice among the Mound Builders, in which the victims—usually volunteers—went to their deaths adorned with mistletoe.

At another site De-coo-dah showed Pidgeon "memorials of migration. . . . Here we behold the six animal effigies, slightly differing in form, symbolizing the migration of the six tribes. . . ." Buffalo and eagle effigies in the group tell the story of quarrels among the tribes, reconciliations, the succession of dynasties, marriages, and a good deal more. One set of mounds constitutes a record of 22 successive sovereigns and the extinction of their line. Another depicts the careers of 96 rulers belonging to six dynasties.

Out of all this there emerges the history of the Elk nation, builders of the mounds. Pidgeon tells the story in such a muddled way that the details are hard to follow, and it is uncertain just who the Elks were—Romans, Persians, Greeks, Hindus—although they clearly were not Indians. De-coo-dah claims to be virtually the last survivor of the Elks, whose downfall and dispersal had occurred shortly before the arrival of Columbus in the New World.

De-coo-dah gives a jumbled account of the civil wars of the Elks "during the reign of the great De-co-ta, who was a usurper, descended from the Black Tortoise nation, which came from the south." Assassinations, revolutions, the destruction of dynasties, the quarrels of "nations" hitherto unknown—all this had a powerful effect on Pidgeon's many readers. It was as though he had unearthed a new *Iliad*. The tale describes the division of the Elk nations among three kings, Red-Deer, Black-Wolf, and Little-Otter, all grandsons of the murdered De-co-ta the Great. "The descendants of Little-Otter," De-coo-dah relates, "were probably the last in the great valley of the Mississippi to relinquish the ancient form of hieroglyphical record. After his death, his kingdom being divided between two chiefs only, its power and resources were not greatly impaired; those two chiefs, the Black-Bear and the Big-Buffalo, being highly honored and esteemed, lived at peace with each other for a long time; and their people not being divided into small bands, continued to erect memorial, matrimonial, and title-mounds, so long as they remained united. . . ." But then "the seeds of war were again sown," and dozens of new mounds were built to mark secessions from the Elk nation. In a final conflict the quarreling chiefs destroyed one another and the survivors dispersed in small tribal bands." De-coo-dah declared, "After this final dispersion of the northern tribes, monumental commemorations ceased. The mound being the hieroglyphical sign through which the traditions were taught, and the knowledge of past events preserved, gradually losing its importance, came eventually to be looked upon with cold indifference. And thus the great fountain of tradition being dried up, it is by no means matter of wonder that its streams have ceased to flow."

But who *were* the Mound Builders? Pidgeon suggests that the Elks, in the northern part of the United States, may have been of Danish or other European descent. In the South, where flat-topped pyramids were built, the dominant race may have been Mexican. These two races, he argues, collided near the junction of the Missouri and Mississippi

10 An Ancient American battlemound. Engraving from
Traditions of De-Coo-Dah, by William Pidgeon, 1858.

rivers, and weakened each other so much in warfare that
they both were an easy prey to the wandering hordes of red
men out of Asia who conquered them. Finally, so he claims,
a great flood swept over the whole eastern half of the continent and engulfed the surviving Mound Builders.

Traditions of De-coo-dah is a crazy masterpiece of
pseudoscience, a glib entangling of virtually every myth
that had been told about the Mound Builders. Though

everything in it was pure nonsense, Pidgeon was audacious enough to offer his manuscript originally to the Smithsonian for publication in the *Contributions to Knowledge* series; it was indignantly rejected, whereupon Pidgeon gave it to a commercial publisher and made a fortune. For twenty years laymen read it with fascination, and archaeologists found bitter amusement in its idiocies; but then for a brief while it acquired a kind of scientific respectability.

This process began in 1875 with *Native Races of the Pacific States,* a five-volume work by H. H. Bancroft of San Francisco. This merchant-turned-historian used platoons of anonymous assistants to help him in his writing, and occasionally some odd things slipped through—as in his reference to the effigy mounds of Wisconsin, "on which Lapham and Pidgeon are the prominent authorities." A. J. Conant's *Footprints of Vanished Races* (1879) reproduced five of Pidgeon's diagrams of geometrical earthworks, three of his plans of effigy mounds, and a good many of his "traditions." Pidgeon was used as a source by several other scholarly writers in the next few years.

But apparently no one had actually gone to Wisconsin to see if the mounds Pidgeon had written about existed. That job was undertaken in 1884 by T. H. Lewis of St. Paul, Minnesota, a surveyor, who reported on his findings in the January 1886 issue of *The American Journal of Archaeology.* Lewis went looking for Pidgeon's "Monumental Tortoise" mounds on the Minnesota River, described as an "extensive group of tumuli and embankments." After a thorough search, Lewis found a group of mounds at approximately the place Pidgeon had given. The resemblance between what Pidgeon claimed to have seen and what Lewis saw was non-existent. "His heights and dimensions," wrote Lewis, "were undoubtedly mere estimates, and very poor ones at that. But how account for mounds of shapes so radically different from those that any other man ever heard of before or since our author's time? Or why so many more mounds represented than actually exist immediately around this central mound or tortoise?"

Lewis visited and surveyed other mound groups mentioned by Pidgeon in Wisconsin and Iowa, and interviewed many old settlers who remembered him. "I do not want to be understood as charging Mr. Pidgeon with a deliberate and intentional fabrication of arrangements and conformations of earthworks," Lewis declared. "But I have reason to know that it is not safe to quote his statements as authority." And he concluded emphatically, "The result of all my researches in this respect is to convince me that the Elk nation and its last prophet De-coo-dah are modern myths, which have never had any objective existence; and that, consequently, the ancient history in the volume is of no more account than that of the Lost Tribes in the Book of Mormon."

7

The great debate over the Mound Builders raged on through the 1850's and 1860's. Throughout the world the modern era in archaeology was beginning, and public interest in the new discoveries ran high. The clang of picks and shovels was heard everywhere. In Egypt, the secrets of the Pharaohs were being laid bare. In Mesopotamia, a dashing young man named Austen Henry Layard had begun in 1845 to dig along the Tigris River, and shortly announced to a dazzled world that he had unearthed the Assyrian city of Nineveh.

Charles Darwin's *Origin of Species,* offering the revolutionary idea that the appearance of living things could change or "evolve" over many generations, was published in 1859. Two years before, the discovery of a strange-looking human skull at a place in Germany called Neanderthal had provided evidence of a possible earlier type of man. Archbishop Ussher's calculation that the world had been created in 4004 B.C. was discredited. And still the archae-

ological revolution went on. In 1870, Heinrich Schliemann
began to uncover Homer's Troy, while other men planned
work in Syria, Crete, and the Holy Land.

It was a confusing, exciting time, when old concepts were
swept away with each morning's newspapers, and the past
suddenly seemed uncertain and changeable. The public demanded books that would bring some order into the chaos
of the new ideas of antiquity.

The notion that the world was many thousands or even
millions of years old was stunning and disturbing. The related idea that man himself was ancient, and had passed
through several evolutionary stages on the way to his present
form, was even more upsetting. Those who believed in
vanished Mound Builders, though, welcomed the new time-
scheme. Suddenly there was room in the past for all sorts
of forgotten empires. It was possible, said the enthusiasts,
that tens of thousands of years had elapsed since the downfall of the Mound Builders and the arrival of the American
Indians.

The archaeological findings coming from the Old World
helped to support this idea. Egypt and Mesopotamia were
yielding skeletons, mummies, and works of art known to
be at least twenty-five hundred years old, in an almost
perfect state of preservation. But the skeletons and artifacts
found in the American mounds were often crumbling into
dust. This seemed to prove that the mounds were more
ancient than the Old World sites. Actually it was not age,
but the difference between the desert climate of the Near
East and the temperate climate of North America, that accounted for the better state of preservation of the Old
World finds; but no one thought of that at first.

One of the most successful of the new popular books on

American prehistory was John D. Baldwin's *Ancient America,* published in 1872. This well-illustrated volume covered the Incas of Peru, the various Mexican civilizations, the Pueblos, and the Mound Builders; and, with an emphasis typical of its era, devoted some two hundred of its three hundred pages to the mounds. "Careful study of what is shown in the many reports on these ancient remains," Baldwin wrote, "seems plainly to authorize the conclusion that the Mound-Builders entered the country at the South, and began their settlements near the Gulf." He felt that "the Mound-Builders had a certain degree of civilization which raised them far above the condition of savages," and doubted that they were related to the American Indians. A race that has sunk to barbarism after being civilized retains some traditions of its past greatness, Baldwin points out, but he insists that the Indians had always been barbarians: "There was nothing to indicate that either the Indians inhabiting our part of the continent, or their ancestors near or remote, had ever been civilized, even to the extent of becoming capable of settled life and organized industry." He rejects all such legends as Heckewelder's tale of the Tallegewi: "The traditionary lore of the wild Indians had nothing to say of the Mound-Builders, who appear to have been as unknown and mysterious to these Indians as they are to us."

Baldwin believed that the Mound Builders were an ancient race, citing as proof such things as tree-ring counts and the extreme condition of decay of the skeletons found in the mounds. Since it seemed to him that it must have taken an extraordinarily long time to create the earthworks of the Mississippi Valley, and that the disappearance of the Mound Builders had occurred hundreds of years ago, their original arrival at the Gulf of Mexico must have come at an extremely early date.

Baldwin dismisses most of the wilder theories of the Mound Builders' origin, such as the Lost Tribes of Israel theory, which he calls "a lunatic fancy," and of which he says, "Nothing can be more unwarranted or more absurd." That Phoenician voyagers may have reached the Americas appears quite reasonable to him, but if they were the founders of early American civilization, he points out, "it would be true also that they built in America as they never built any-where else, that they established a language here radically unlike their own, and that they used a style of writing totally different from that which they carried into every other region occupied by their colonies." He uses similar logic against other imaginative hypotheses.

His conclusion is that the Mound Builders "were unques-tionably American aborigines, and not immigrants from another continent." He suggested "that the Mound-Builders came originally from Mexico and Central America. It ex-plains many facts connected with their remains. In the Great Valley [of the Mississippi] their most populous settle-ments were at the south. Coming from Mexico and Central America, they would begin their settlements on the Gulf coast, and afterward advance gradually up the river to the Ohio Valley."

The possibility that the Northern people were merely influenced by Mexican traits of which they had somehow learned was evidently too subtle for 1872. Baldwin com-pares the stone pyramids of Yucatán and the earthen pyra-mids of the United States and uses them to prove actual Mexican migration. "The high mounds also in the two regions are remarkably alike," he says. "In both cases they are pyramidal in shape, and have level summits of considerable extent, which were reached by means of stairways on the outside." Relating the Grave Creek and Miamisburg (Ohio) mounds to three Mayan pyramids in Mexico, he declares, "All these mounds were constructed for religious uses, and they are, in their way, as much alike as any five Gothic churches."

But he did not think the Mayans and the Mound Builders were one. Instead he related the Mound Builders to a different Mexican people—the mysterious Toltecs, who, he observes, "are said to have come into the country [Mexico] about a thousand years before the Christian era. Their supremacy appears to have ceased, and left the country broken up into small states, two or three centuries before the Aztecs appeared." He quotes a Mexican tradition of "an ancient empire known as Huehue-Tlapalan," from which the Toltecs migrated to Mexico, and suggests that Huehue-Tlapalan was located in the Mississippi and Ohio valleys, where he thinks the Toltecs lived and built earthworks before they conquered Mexico.

But earlier Baldwin had said that the Mound Builders were emigrants *from* Mexico who landed on the Gulf Coast and spread northward up the Mississippi. So to make his Toltec theory hold up he has to imagine a double migration. First, in the really remote past, an ancient Mexican culture sent colonists to the Mississippi Valley. After a long residence there, during which they built pyramids and ramparts of earth, these colonists—the Toltecs—returned to Mexico, "so much changed in speech and other respects as to seem a distinct people," and conquered their ancestral country.

The reason for leaving the Mississippi Valley, according to Baldwin, was invasion by barbarians; he feels that the Toltecs abandoned Ohio in distant antiquity, but maintained settlements along the Gulf of Mexico until relatively recent times.

Another book that won a wide public at this period was J. W. Foster's *Prehistoric Races of the United States of America,* published in 1873. Foster, president of the Chicago Academy of Sciences, was a geographer who became enthralled by the Mound Builders when "for the first time I gazed upon the works of that mysterious people" at Newark, Ohio. His approach is modern; he is very much aware of living in an era when startling revelations have overthrown old conceptions of the past. In his first sentence he declares; "The combined investigations of geologists and ethnologists, prosecuted during the last quarter of a century, have thrown much light upon the origin of the human race, and developed facts which require us to essentially modify our pre-existing views as to the length of time during which it has occupied our planet." He is bold enough to claim that mankind has existed "through thousands of generations"—a flat contradiction of orthodox religious belief. Even among scientists Foster was well ahead of his time in accepting such ideas.

But in discussing the Indians and the Mound Buliders, he still clings to the myth of the Mound Builders as a separate race. "The Indian possesses a conformation of skull which clearly separates him from the pre-historic Mound Builder," Foster asserts, thus coming to a conclusion exactly opposite from that reached by the anatomist Samuel G. Morton some 30 years earlier. Not only skull shape but also differences in ability mark the Indians off from the Mound Builders; for Foster, like most Americans of the day, simply could not believe the Indian capable of building the mounds:

"His character, since first known to the white man has been signalized by treachery and cruelty. He repels all efforts to raise him from his degraded position: and whilst he has not the moral nature to adopt the virtues of civilization, his brutal instincts lead him to welcome its vices. He was never known voluntarily to engage in an enterprise requiring methodical labor; he dwells in temporary and movable habitations; he follows the game in their migrations; he imposes the drudgery of life upon his squaw; he takes no heed for the future. To suppose that such a race threw up the strong lines of circumvallation and the symmetrical mounds which crown so many of our river-terraces, is as preposterous, almost, as to suppose that they built the pyramids of Egypt."

Actually, of course, many American Indian tribes had rich and complex cultures, different from but not necessarily inferior to that of the white man. Where Indians were shiftless, drunken, or vicious, it was usually a result of the oppression brought upon them by European conquerors. But this was hard to understand in Foster's time. Then, the Indians stood in the way of the growth of the United States, and it was simplest to regard them as worthless, brutish savages. To "prove" that the lowly Indians could not possibly have built the wondrous mounds of the Ohio and Mississippi valleys was part of the political campaign aimed at wiping these people out in the name of American progress.

The Neanderthal skull, with its low forehead and jutting brows, also had its influence on Foster's thinking. Using skulls from mounds in Iowa, Illinois, and Indiana, Foster jumped to the conclusion that all Mound Builders had thick, massive heads, with low, flat foreheads and enormous ridges over the eyes—in fact, characteristics not very different from those of the Neanderthal specimen. These studies, he wrote, "have led me to infer that the Mound-Builders' crania were characterized by a general conformation of parts, which clearly separated them from the existing races of man, and particularly from the Indians of North America."

As Foster discusses the Mound Builder "race," he drifts into an odd paradox. He has set out to show that a basic difference, both physical and mental, separates the diligent, well-organized, productive Mound Builders from the lazy, drunken, savage American Indians. But in describing the physical traits of the earlier race he reports that "no one, I think, can view this fragment of a [mound] skull . . . without coming to the conclusion that its possessor was a ferocious brute," and he ends by declaring, "All the [mound] specimens indicate a low intellectual organization, little removed from that of the idiot."

Where, then, are the "superior" Mound Builders?

Dr. Foster has an ingenious answer. "The Mound-builders, assuming these skulls to be typical, were doubtless neither eminent for great virtues nor great vices," he declares, "but were a mild, inoffensive race, who would fall an easy prey to a crafty and cruel foe. Under the guidance of a superior mind, we can imagine that they would be content to toil, without weighing deliberately the nature or amount of the reward. Like the Chinese, they could probably imitate but not invent; and, secure from the irruption of enemies, they would, in time, develop a rude civilization."

Thus he turns the glorious Mound Builders into the docile, dull-witted Mound Builders, who placidly erect their colossal ramparts to gratify ambitious prehistoric overseers whose own skulls have somehow failed to reach Dr. Foster's laboratory. It was, at any rate, a different approach.

8

The more that was published about the Mound Builders, the more passionate the debate grew, and the more energetically the archaeologists, both professional and amateur, searched for new evidence. Not all the excavation was scientific in intent, of course. In 1879 and 1880, the inhabitants of Charlestown, Missouri, learned that the handsome pottery found in their local mounds could bring high prices from Eastern collectors. "A regular mining fever at once broke out," one archaeologist reported, "and spread so rapidly that in some instances as many as twenty-five or thirty men, women and children could be seen digging for pottery in one field at the same time. The specimens obtained were taken to Charlestown and sold to merchants, who in turn sold them to various museums, scientific institutions, and relic hunters. It is said that this trade brought to town several thousand dollars."

In the course of amateur activity some evidence appeared concerning one of the most interesting sidelights of the Mound Builder controversy: the extinct prehistoric animals of the Americas. The bones of the extinct elephantlike creatures known as mammoths and mastodons had been discovered in the eighteenth century, along with fossils of giant ground sloths and other relics of vanished creatures. Everyone agreed that these animals must have died out in the distant past; the question was whether man had existed in the Americas at the time they roamed.

In 1838, a professional dealer in fossils named Albert Koch found a site in Missouri where the charred bones of a mastodon lay near broken spears, axes, and stone knives, very much as though the huge beast had been slaughtered and roasted for a prehistoric barbecue. This was the first time that anyone had come upon human relics associated with mastodon remains; but Koch was not considered trustworthy by most scientists, and no one took his find seriously. Several other sites that seemed to prove that man and mastodon had been contemporaries turned up in the years that followed, but these, too, were ignored by cautious scientists.

In 1874, Jared Warner of Wyalusing, Wisconsin, sent the Smithsonian a drawing of an effigy mound on his property that appeared to have the form of an elephant. The animal

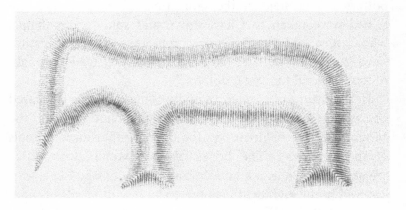

11   Wisconsin elephant mound. Engraving from the *Second Annual Report of the Bureau of Ethnology.*

depicted was 133 feet long, and had a "trunk" 31 feet in length. Skeptics pointed out that the "elephant mound" had neither tusks nor tail, and that the "trunk" might have been the result of flood waters adding earth to a bear-effigy mound. Others, though, interpreted the mound as an ancient portrait of a mastodon.

More bitterly-contested discoveries of the same sort were made in and about Davenport, Iowa: two "elephant pipes" and three remarkable inscribed tablets. They came to light in a group of mounds on the bank of the Mississippi about a mile south of the city. The Reverend Jacob Gass, a Lutheran clergyman of Davenport, had found and partly excavated these mounds in 1874, finding in them deftly carved stone pipes and various copper axes and spools. In 1877, he dug in the Davenport mounds again, aided by two students. Beneath a layer of modern relics—glass beads and fragments of a brass ring—Gass found a layer of shells twelve or fifteen inches thick. Below this was loose black soil with fragments of human bones in it; and at the bottom, five and a half feet below the top of the mound, they unearthed two inscribed tablets lying close together on a hard clay floor.

The larger tablet, twelve inches long and eight to ten inches wide, was made of dark slate. It had a scene on each side. One face showed a fire burning on the summit of a mound, a number of bodies lying about it as if awaiting cremation, and a group of supposed Mound Builders standing in a circle. Above this picture were hieroglyphics and letters, including some modern ones; the figure 8 was repeated three times, the letter O seven times, and F and N were also to be seen; other letters resembled Phoenician or Hebrew characters. On the other side was shown a hunting scene, including bison, deer, hares, birds, goats, fish, and three animals that might have been mastodons or possibly moose. Of the eight human figures in the scene, one was wearing a hat with a brim.

The smaller tablet, seven inches square, became known as "the calendar stone." It contained twelve signs within three concentric circles. The signs seemed to resemble the signs of the zodiac. A third inscribed tablet was discovered a year after the first two. Once again the Reverend Mr. Gass was present, though the actual discoverer was Charles Harrison, the president of the Davenport Academy of Natural Sciences. Beneath a stone slab in the mound was a stone vault, in which Harrison found a small quartz crystal, a shell, four arrow points, and a limestone tablet one and a half inches thick. Engraved on the tablet were a crescent (the moon?), a circle (the sun?), and a human figure colored bright red (a sun-god?). A figure 8 and other characters were inscribed on the tablet, along with the outlines of a bird, an animal, and an ax, all quite crudely drawn.

Two years later, in 1880, Gass and another Lutheran minister, the Reverend Ad Blumer, made another unusual discovery in a different mound group near Davenport. It was a pipe on which was mounted an image of a clumsy-looking animal with a long snout. No tusks were visible; but everyone began speaking of it as an "elephant pipe." Blumer, the discoverer, gave it to the Davenport Academy of Natural Sciences.

Shortly the Academy acquired another such pipe, which in fact had been discovered first. As W. H. Pratt, then the president of the Academy, reported in 1882, "The first elephant pipe, which we obtained a little more than a year ago, was found some six years before by an illiterate German farmer named Peter Mare, while planting corn on a farm in the mound region, Louisa County, Iowa. He did not care whether it was elephant or kangaroo; to him it was a curious 'Indian stone,' and nothing more, and he kept it and smoked it. In 1878 he removed to Kansas, and when he left he gave the pipe to his brother-in-law, a farm laborer, who also smoked it. Mr. Gass happened to hear of it, as he is always inquiring about such things, hunted up the man and borrowed the pipe to take photographs and casts from it. He could not buy it. The man said his brother-in-law gave it to him and as it was a curious thing—he wanted to keep it. We were, however, unfortunate, or fortunate, enough to break it; that spoiled it for him and that was his chance to make some money out of it. He could have claimed any amount, and we would, as in duty bound, have raised it for him, but he was satisfied with three or four dollars." The elephant shown on this pipe was similar to Blumer's find, but much more massive of body, with a pronounced trunk curled back almost to its forelegs.

The opinion of most scientists of 1880 was that the mammoth and the mastodon had vanished from the Americas thousands of years before. Perhaps—as the charred bones of the Koch find and others seemed to show—the most primitive inhabitants of the New World had hunted them; perhaps not. But on the evidence of the Davenport pipes and tablet, it now seemed that Mound Builders had been contemporaries of those ancient beasts. That seemed to prove that the gap in time between the Mound Builders and the American Indians must have been huge. The existence of the Mound Builders as a distinct, ancient, and vanished race had seemingly been established. The voices of those who credited the mounds to the ancestors of recent Indian tribesmen were drowned out.

But then a new voice was heard across the land: that of the Smithsonian Institution. And what had seemed like fact in 1880 was transformed into myth by 1890.

▲▲▲ 5

DEFLATING THE MYTH

▲▲▲

John Wesley Powell, who had so much to do with demythologizing the American mounds, first encountered them as a boy in Ohio. He was born in 1834, the son of a Wesleyan preacher; his birthplace was near Palmyra, New York, where Joseph Smith supposedly had found the golden plates of Mormon. In gradual stages the Powells moved westward until they settled in Jackson, Ohio, not far from Chillicothe.

Jackson was a community of about 250 people, with six stores and three taverns. Among its citizens was George Crookham, a successful farmer, a self-taught amateur scientist, and an enemy of slavery, who regularly helped escaping slaves reach freedom. Crookham and the Powells had much in common: eager minds, love of learning, and a willingness to accept unpopular ideas. Hatred of slavery drew the Powells and Crookham together, and George Crookham became virtually a second father to young John Wesley Powell.

It was Crookham who gave the future director of the Smithsonian Institution's Bureau of American Ethnology his first look at the earthworks of Ohio. He was a kind of

unofficial schoolmaster, who taught, without fee, local boys
wishing to improve themselves. He owned a two-room log
cabin in which he kept his collections of plants, animals,
and Indian relics, his library, and his chemical apparatus.
Young Wes Powell was one of his best pupils. On his walk-
ing tours with Crookham he collected crawfish and min-
nows, pried fossils from rocks, and examined unusual
geological formations. He also dug in the mounds of
Chillicothe, finding and treasuring flint points and other
artifacts, while Crookham explained to him what was known
about the Mound Builders in 1844.

Then a gang of pro-slavery hoodlums burned down
Crookham's little museum, and the Powells began to think
of moving on. In the summer of 1846 they left Ohio for
South Grove, Wisconsin. Here Wes Powell met the peaceful,
friendly Winnebago Indians, who had been badly treated
by the white men; as he watched the Winnebagos fishing
and feasting, he began to develop his powerful, passionate
sympathy for Indian life.

In 1851 the Powells moved again, this time to northern
Illinois. Wes, now 17, found a job as a schoolmaster at $14
a month. He taught arithmetic, geology, and geography,
and taught himself geometry so he could teach it, lesson by
lesson, to the pupils who followed a step or two behind him.
His father had helped to found a college in Wheaton, Illinois, and Powell went to enroll there in December 1853.
But he turned away bitterly when he discovered that no
courses in science or mathematics were offered. He continued teaching school, and in his spare time went on field
trips to excavate mounds or to collect fossils and shells. On
one trip he traveled nearly the whole length of the Mississippi alone in a small rowboat. He also picked up a sketchy

college education through brief stays at several schools, but mainly he was his own teacher, attaining a deep knowledge of geology, archaeology, and natural history.

From 1858 to 1860 he spent much time in and around the mounds of Ohio, Indiana, Illinois, and Missouri. At that time he shared the widely held view that the mounds and other earthworks of the eastern half of the United States were relics of an ancient people far more advanced than the Indians. But the more he dug, the more doubtful of this he grew. In the fall of 1859 Powell excavated some mounds on the shore of Lake Peoria, Illinois, finding in one of them skeletons and artifacts. He wrote many years later: "At the bottom, with some articles of pottery, shells, stone implements, etc., an ornament was found made of copper skillfully cut in imitation of a spread eagle, with head turned to one side. Lying by the side of this were a few glass beads. These challenged attention, and the question was necessarily presented to him [Powell speaking of himself], Did these ancient people have the art of making glass? . . . If these articles were the work of the mound-builders in pre-Columbian times, then the people must have possessed arts more advanced than those shown by the mound arts previously studied. Thus a suspicion arose as to the correctness of the prevailing opinion."

These investigations were interrupted by the Civil War. Powell enlisted as a private in the Union Army, and rose through the ranks to become a major. While campaigning in Missouri, Tennessee, and Mississippi, however, Powell found time to examine many groups of mounds. He reported later that "most of the works of art unearthed were of stone, bone, shell, and pottery, but in excavating a mound with stone graves near Nashville, Tennessee, more glass beads were discovered and also an iron knife, very much rusted. . . . At the time of this find his former suspicion became a hypothesis that the mounds from which the glass, copper, and iron articles were taken were constructed subsequent to the advent of the white man on this continent, and that the contents gave evidence of barter between the civilized and savage races."

In the battle of Shiloh, in 1862, Powell suffered a wound that cost him his left arm. Despite this, he quickly returned to duty, and even insisted on taking his bride of six months into the battle zone. At the end of the war Powell became a professor of geology at Illinois Wesleyan University, and before long he was off on summer field trips to the Rocky Mountains with his classes. These expeditions led to his astonishing river journey in 1869 through the Grand Canyon; the one-armed major, accompanied by students and mountain men, shot the rapids of the turbulent Colorado River with true heroism and successfully carried out one of the most important exploring trips in American history. On the strength of this achievement Powell became a nationally known figure and was made Director of the United States Geological Survey, with responsibility for supervising the exploration of the entire western half of the continent.

Throughout his years of geological study, Major Powell retained his early interest in archaeology and in ethnology, the study of living peoples. On his expeditions to the West he collected examples of Indian garments, weapons, and pottery, and made notes on the languages of various tribes. He realized that it was virtually the last chance to record the details of these vanishing cultures, and he felt a powerful conviction that such details *were* worth recording. In

1877 he produced a pioneering work of high importance, *Introduction to the Study of Indian Languages,* which established him as a professional ethnologist of the first rank.

A year later, in a report to the Secretary of the Interior, Powell asked for the creation of a government agency to carry on research on the Indians. "The field of research is speedily narrowing," he wrote, "because of the rapid change in the Indian population now in progress; all habits, customs, and opinions are fading away; even languages are disappearing; and in a very few years it will be impossible to study our North American Indians in their primitive condition, except from recorded history. For this reason ethnologic studies in America should be pushed with the utmost vigor." He argued that much of the conflict between white man and Indian in the United States could have been avoided if there had been more knowledge of Indian ways: "The blunders we have made and the wrongs we have inflicted upon the Indians . . . have been cruel and inexcusable, except on the ground of our ignorance."

Powell, the war hero and famous explorer, had enough influence in Congress to get his request approved. In March 1879, Congress set aside $20,000 for the publication of the material on American Indians that the U. S. Geological Survey had collected. The Smithsonian Institution was assigned the task of preparing this material, through a new department called the Bureau of Ethnology (later known as the Bureau of American Ethnology). Powell was named director of the Bureau of Ethnology; another man took charge of the Geological Survey, but poor health forced him to resign within two years, and after 1881 Powell headed both bureaus. Thereafter he was an extremely busy man in the nation's capital.

2

With what even then was a very slim budget, Powell led the Smithsonian into the active study of the American Indians. Congress had meant the $20,000 merely to cover the cost of completing and publishing certain ethnological material already on hand, but Powell interpreted things differently and conjured up a permanent research department. He hired a small staff and lined up the beginnings of what would eventually be a far-flung network of part-time field investigators.

Powell did not see the work of his bureau as archaeological; he planned only to study the languages, arts, institutions, and mythologies of existing tribes, and originally had no intention of using Bureau of Ethnology funds for excavating mounds or ruins. This is evident from the First Annual Report of the Bureau of Ethnology, dated July 1880 and published the following year. This huge volume includes essays on Indian languages, myths, and burial customs, on Central American picture writing, and several other subjects; but only 8 of its 638 pages are devoted to mounds. In one of his own essays Powell declares that there seems no reason to search for a lost race of Mound Builders; to him the mounds appear quite clearly to be the work of ancestors of the modern Indians. In a quiet, offhand way, Major Powell thus sounded the first battle cry of the coming revolution in American archaeology. On the same page he suggested discarding the concept of a single race of Mound Builders; "the wide extent and vast number of mounds discovered in the United States should lead us to suspect, at least, that the mound-builders of pre-historic times belonged to many and diverse stocks."

Though he had no plans to deal with the mounds, Powell found an odd thing happening the next time Congress voted money for his bureau, in 1881. A group of archaeologists, without telling him, persuaded Congress to decree that of the $25,000 being given the bureau for further research, $5,000 must be spent in "continuing . . . investigation relating to mound-builders and prehistoric mounds."

Powell was not very pleased. He wanted to use all the money he could get to study living tribes, and was upset at being forced by Congress to branch out into archaeology. But he obeyed the order, and set up a division of mound investigation within the bureau. Late in 1881 he chose as head of this division Cyrus Thomas, a botanist and geologist, who was destined to be the slayer of the Mound Builder myth.

Thomas came from the southern tip of Illinois, where mounds were common. He was a man of wide interests who had somehow acquired the title of "professor." When he came to the Bureau of Ethnology he was, he said, "a pronounced believer in the existence of a race of Mound Builders, distinct from the American Indians." Major Powell proposed to cure him of this belief by putting him in charge of the bureau's mound work and letting him convince himself of his error. Powell gave Professor Thomas one clerk and three field assistants and told him to draw up a plan for a survey of the mounds.

Gradually the bureau's main interest, as shown in its annual reports, shifted from ethnology to archaeology. The Second Annual Report, submitted in September 1882, includes an essay entitled, "Animal Carvings from Mounds of the Mississippi Valley," which was Powell's first real blast in the war against the mound myth. Its author was Henry W. Henshaw, an expert on birds, who had not actually excavated any mounds himself and who was merely attacking some of the conclusions drawn by earlier writers about mounds.

In a preface to Henshaw's piece, Powell plainly indicates what the position of his bureau on the mounds is going to be. He denounces "the many false statements" and the "contradictions and absurdities" of many supposed authorities on the mounds, and asserts that "the garbling and perversion of the lower class of writers supplemented the phantasies of those better intentioned."

The discovery of the mounds of the Mississippi basin, Powell goes on, opened "a new field . . . to enthusiastic theorists. Ignoring the fact that many of the historic Indians have practiced the building of mounds, indeed that some are still building them, it was assumed that these works were the vestiges of a dense and extinct population whose advance in civilization was much superior to that of the known American Indians. From the size and forms of their mounds, their location, and the objects contained in them, writers have set forth the origin, migrations, numbers, institutions, art, and religions of their builders. . . . But those who have hitherto conducted the researches . . . were swept by blind zeal into serious errors even when they were not imposed upon by frauds and forgeries."

Then Henshaw takes over for a brisk demolition job. The first target is the revered Ephraim George Squier and his colleague, Dr. Davis. Tactfully Henshaw pays homage to "the skill and zeal" of Squier and Davis and to "the ability and fidelity which marks the presentation of their results

12 Manatee pipe, after Squier and Davis. Engraving from the *Second Annual Report of the Bureau of Ethnology.*

13 Manatee. Engraving from the *Second Annual Report of the Bureau of Ethnology.*

to the public." Then he falls on them for having been too imaginative in interpreting the animal effigies seen on carved pipes from the mound. Squier had claimed that several pipes showed manatees, large seal-like animals found only in tropical waters; the presence of manatee pipes in the Ohio mounds seemed to indicate the existence of some sort of trade route linking Ohio and the tropical shores of Florida, and even the possibility of a far-flung empire. Other pipes, according to Squier and Davis, showed the big-beaked tropical birds known as toucans, giving further support to the theory of a highly developed, far-reaching Mound Builder civilization.

Henshaw, the professional naturalist, showed that Squier's manatees and toucans were really only otters and crows; therefore the pipes did not prove contact with tropical regions at all. The curious thing is that although he was right about the species involved, he was wrong about the basic point; for we know today, from archaeological evidence, that Ohio *was* connected by trade routes with many distant parts of North America, including Florida, at the time when the mounds were being built. But Henshaw's blast had the value of correcting falsely interpreted evidence—even if the false interpretation had accidentally provided a correct answer!

Henshaw attacks the incorrect conclusions of several other highly respected writers, such as Sir Daniel Wilson, author of *Prehistoric Man: Researches into the origin of*

14   Raven pipe from Mound City. Courtesy Ohio Historical Society, Columbus, Ohio.

15 Toucan, after Squier and Davis. Engraving from the *Second Annual Report of the Bureau of Ethnology.*

civilization in the old and new world. Wilson, the man who coined the word "prehistoric," had used the supposed manatee and toucan pipes to argue that the Mound Builders had emigrated from Mexico or Central America, "bringing with them the arts of the tropics, and models derived from the animals familiar to their fathers in the parentland of the race." He had also cited certain ornaments found in the Ohio mounds that were made of the shell of the conch, a giant sea snail which Wilson believed lived only in tropical waters thousands of miles from Ohio. Henshaw simply remarks that conchs have been found in the United States as far north as North Carolina, while a similar animal known to the Mound Builders and often confused with the conch by archaeologists is found as far north as Massachusetts.

As a zoologist, Henshaw reserves his sharpest barbs for those who claimed to see evidence of a relationship between Mound Builders and mastodons. Wisconsin's "elephant mound" strikes him as no more than a bear effigy to which an accidental trunk has been attached by flood action. He is even less generous to the two elephant pipes of Davenport, Iowa. These he considers fakes, although he does not quite use that ugly word; he also wonders why no attempt was made to indicate tusks in these pipes, since a primitive artist would certainly have been impressed by such a conspicuous feature of mastodons.

The fact that the Reverend Jacob Gass was involved in the discovery of both elephant pipes and also the inscribed Davenport tablets seems strange to Henshaw: "Archaeologists must certainly deem it unfortunate that outside of the Wisconsin [elephant] mound the only evidence of the coexistence of the Mound-Builder and the mastodon should reach the scientific world through the agency of one individual." Instead of strengthening faith in the earlier discoveries, the later ones by the same man merely created "ever increasing suspicion," said Henshaw. As we shall see, these remarks created no little anger in Davenport, Iowa.

Henshaw's conclusions amounted to a summary of the Powell position on the mounds. He wrote that no carvings had been found in the mounds that represented animals not native to the Mississippi Valley; that "the state of art-culture reached by the Mound Builders, as illustrated by their carvings, has been greatly overestimated"; and that "the theories of origin for the Mound Builders suggested by the presence in the mounds of carvings of supposed foreign animals are without basis."

3

The Third Annual Report of the Bureau of Ethnology, published in 1884, included for the first time a brief section entitled, "Explorations in Mounds." It discusses work done in West Virginia, Ohio, Tennessee, Arkansas, and Florida. Another piece in the same volume was a well-illustrated catalog of artifacts found in mounds of North Carolina, Tennessee, and Arkansas. This reproduced a number of strikingly handsome works of ceramic art, showing that at least in the Southeast the Mound Builders had been unusually gifted potters. The commentary accompanying these illustrations was the work of William Henry Holmes, a talented painter who had given up art for geology, then had drifted into archaeology, and was serving Powell ably both in the Geological Survey and in the Bureau of Ethnology.

By 1883, Cyrus Thomas's Division of Mound Explorations included three full-time assistants and five temporary helpers, and work was under way in Tennessee, Arkansas, Illinois, Iowa, Georgia, Alabama, North Carolina, and Missouri. Some 4,100 artifacts had been collected for the National Museum in Washington. They included elegant pipes and pendants of polished stones and such humbler things as hoes, scrapers, diggers, axes, and hammers. Some of the mounds had yielded clear evidence of contact with European civilization: bits of hammered iron in North Carolina; silver bracelets, brooches, and crosses in Wisconsin, and fragments of copper plate bearing the marks of machinery in Illinois. All this served to back Powell's original belief that "a few, at least, of the important mounds of the valley of the Mississippi, had been constructed and used subsequent to the occupation of the continent by Europeans, and that some, at least, of the mound builders were therefore none other than known Indian tribes."

The Fourth Annual Report contains an essay by Garrick Mallery on the picture-writing of the Indians, in which he discusses the various inscribed tablets found in mounds.

Most of these he dismisses as frauds, such as the one found by David Wyrick of Newark, Ohio, "who, to prove his theory that the Hebrews were the mound-builders, discovered in 1860 a tablet bearing on one side a truculent 'likeness' of Moses with his name in Hebrew, and on the other a Hebrew abridgement of the ten commandments. A Hebrew bible afterwards found in Mr. Wyrick's private room threw some light on the inscribed characters." Apparently Newark was a center for the manufacture of fake mound tablets, mostly intended for sale to tourists.

Mallery did not include the Davenport, Iowa, tablets in his attack, except to suggest that they should be regarded with some caution. But the damage was already done; Iowa was up in arms over Henshaw's comments about the Reverend Jacob Gass, and early in 1885 came a fiery counterblast from Iowa. It took the form of a slender pamphlet by Charles E. Putnam, that year's president of the Davenport Academy of Natural Sciences, entitled *A Vindication of the Authenticity of the Elephant Pipes and Inscribed Tablets in the Museum of the Davenport Academy of Natural Sciences, from the Accusations of the Bureau of Ethnology of the Smithsonian Institution.*

The small-town scholars struck back vigorously against the big government-sponsored research bureau in Washington. "In the sharp controversy now being waged among archaeologists, as to the origin of the Mound-builders," Putnam begins, "the Bureau of Ethnology connected with the Smithsonian Institution has taken a decided position as the champion of the theory that this mysterious race can be traced with comparative certainty to the ancestors of our American Indians." He quotes one of Powell's statements on this topic; then, to provide the opposite side, quotes J. W.

Foster's passage on the savagery and laziness of the American Indian, and cites Squier and Davis on the settled agricultural way of life of the Mound Builders. But the Davenport Academy itself, whose members, Putnam says, are "earnest seekers after truth," has "postponed decision upon these important deductions, awaiting further discoveries."

Putnam has high praise for the "able and accomplished scholars" of the Bureau of Ethnology. But he regrets that in their zeal to establish the theory of the American Indian ancestry of the Mound Builders, some of the bureau's researchers "have sometimes abandoned scientific methods" and "indulged in hasty generalizations." He speaks particularly of Henry W. Henshaw's paper in the Bureau's Second Annual Report, which took advantage of the "commanding position" occupied by the Smithsonian "in the world of science" to deliver "an attack of no ordinary severity . . . upon the Davenport Academy of Natural Sciences."

The Academy, Putnam insists, "has attained deserved eminence" in the field of archaeology. "Its inscribed tablets, elephant pipes, cloth-covered copper axes, and rare collection of ancient pottery have attracted the attention of archaeologists throughout the world of science. These remarkable relics, received with enthusiasm by antiquarians, are generally accepted as authentic additions to the 'unwritten history' of the past." He finds it reasonable "that discoveries so rare and unique should be subjected to severe scrutiny," but objects to Henshaw's hints of fraud.

Concerning the discovery of the pipes and tablets, Putnam says, "The gentlemen engaged in the exploration are well known, and held in high esteem. . . . From the social standing and high character of the principal discoverers, no question has been, or can be, successfully raised as to the authenticity of this discovery." As for the "suspicious" fact that Jacob Gass was involved in all the elephant finds, Putnam quotes another Davenport scholar to the effect that Gass "is a very tireless worker, and not easily discouraged. The mounds in this region are very numerous, but not one in ten contains anything of value. This causes most men to become easily discouraged, but not Mr. Gass. After opening, say, twenty or more mounds without result, he will commence the next with as much vigor as the first. His work is always thorough, and if there is anything to be found he finds it."

16   Davenport elephant pipe. Engraving from *A Vindication of the Authenticity of the Elephant Pipes and Inscribed Tablets,* by Charles E. Putnam, 1885.

Putnam points out that if the Davenport finds are authentic, they constitute strong evidence that man lived in North America while mastodons still existed, and thus that the Mound Builders were an ancient people, "of higher type

and more advanced civilization" than the Indians. "As this
conclusion would conflict with the theory announced by the
Bureau of Ethnology," Putnam writes, "Mr. Henshaw was
compelled to discredit these important discoveries. . . . It
was doubtless unfortunate for the Davenport Academy that
its remarkable discoveries impeded the progress of this
knight-errant of science; but if its elephant pipes and inscribed tablets were authentic and genuine, then his favorite
theory would seem to have been at fault."

Quoting some of Henshaw's "hints, innuendoes, imagin-
ings, suspicions," Putnam attacks him at a vulnerable
point. Henshaw had evidently based his discussion of the
elephant pipes on some sketches of them he had seen in a
magazine; thus he had written that the Davenport elephants
had no tails, though photographs of the actual pipes would
have shown the presence of these appendages. "This ludi-
crous blunder on the part of Mr. Henshaw clearly reveals
the culpable carelessness of his scientific methods," Putnam
declares.

Then he sets forth a long list of evidence proving that
men and mastodons were contemporaries, beginning with
Koch's 1838 discovery of stone axes and arrowheads among
charred mastodon bones in Missouri. Some of this evidence
has been rejected by more recent archaeologists; a good deal
is still accepted; but none of it indicates that mastodons and
Mound Builders were contemporaries, only that mastodons
came under attack from primitive hunters of an unknown
cultural level.

Putnam defends the Reverend Mr. Gass from Henshaw's
implied charge that he was busily planting mastodon carvings all over Iowa. He speaks of Gass' character as "above
reproach," praises his scholarly nature, and says that Gass

"is now preaching to a congregation at Postville, in northern Iowa, where he is, as he everywhere has been, highly esteemed by his people." Putnam attacks Henshaw for having gone outside his own special field—birds—and for trying to act as a dictator to archaeologists.

Putnam strikes the David-and-Goliath theme by contrasting the little Davenport Academy with the wealthy, powerful Smithsonian. He cautions that many specimens in the Smithsonian's own collection may be fakes, since it is able to buy so much that it tempts the dishonest to defraud it, and that the accusations it is hurling against the Davenport artifacts may someday boomerang against some choice item in the Smithsonian.

He sees Powell as a sinister puppet-master using the staff of the Bureau of Ethnology to further his own private theories. He finds it amusing that the ideas Powell is trying to overthrow were published by the Smithsonian itself, in the works of Squier and Davis, among many others. Powell's attack on such works shows, according to Putnam, that the Smithsonian "has not been engaged in the 'diffusion of knowledge' at all, but instead, during all these years, has been scattering error broadcast through the land. We are, therefore, called upon to retrace our steps, to unlearn the lesson we have so long conned, and to take our places at the feet of strange teachers. This is certainly discouraging to American scholarship, and the thoughtful student will wisely pause and make careful inquiry as to which, after all, is error—the earlier or the later deductions."

Time has been unkind to the Davenport relics. In the spring of 1969 the archaeologist Marshall McKusick, of the faculty of the University of Iowa, produced documentary evidence that the inscribed tablets and elephant pipes were frauds, concocted by a few members of the Davenport Academy as a prank on the Reverend Mr. Gass. McKusick revealed that the hoaxers had used broken slates from a building in Davenport. "We had two old almanacs, one German and one Hebrew," one of the pranksters had admitted, "and we copied out of them and inscribed the hieroglyphics on those slate tablets, and things we just made up —anything that would confuse them." The elephant pipes were soaked in oil to make them look ancient. Then the false artifacts were carefully planted where the victims of the hoax were likely to find them. The controversial relics today are owned by the Davenport Public Museum, the successor to the old Davenport Academy of Natural Sciences.

But Charles Putnam's spirited defense, even though it was an unintentional defense of fraud, made a valid point. All too often powerful scientific establishments have, through scorn or suppression, stifled independent thought. Putnam feared that Powell's new Bureau of Ethnology was using its great influence to impose an intellectual tyranny on American archaeology. Even though it happened that the Bureau of Ethnology was closer to the truth about the elephant pipes than was the Davenport Academy, Putnam's fears were correct; in decades to come, on other subjects, the archaeologists who spoke for the Smithsonian were indeed able to impose their ideas on others—and they were not always correct. The cry of outrage from Iowa was a valiant but futile attempt to halt the new juggernaut.

4

While the Bureau of Ethnology toiled to deflate Mound Builder mythology, the mythmakers remained diligent. Now

they were trying to prove that the Mound Builders were
survivors from the lost continent of Atlantis.

Plato had set the Atlantis tale on its way about 355 B.C.
with his dialogue, *Timaeus,* in which is told a story supposedly brought to Greece by travelers who had heard it in
Egypt. It concerns an island larger than Asia and Africa
put together, called Atlantis, which attempted to conquer
Greece and Egypt nine thousand years before Plato's time.
But the Atlanteans were defeated, and soon afterward "there
occurred violent earthquakes and floods, and in a single day
and night of rain . . . the island of Atlantis disappeared, and
was sunk beneath the sea."

In a second work, *Critias,* Plato provided some further
details about the lost continent. It had been, he declared, a
place of great splendor, with soaring palaces, vast canals,
and majestic bridges. One temple, 600 feet long and 300
feet wide, was entirely covered by silver, and its roof was of
gold. There were gardens, racetracks, parks, superb harbors
thronged with ships, wealth beyond measure. And all this
had gone to the bottom of the sea in a single day and night.

Plato's Atlantis was fiction. But the fable took on life of
its own in the centuries that followed. When European sea-
men began venturing into the Atlantic in the fifteenth and
sixteenth centuries, there were frequent reports that the
remnants of the lost continent had been sighted; and when
they reached South and Central America and found the
highly developed, civilized Aztecs, Mayas, and Incas, it
was easy to conclude that they were descendants of refugees
from that great land.

Many writers discussed Atlantis and offered theories
about its destruction and its possible survivors. The one who

connected it with the Mound Builders was Ignatius T. T. Donnelly (1831–1901), a native of Philadelphia, who in 1856 moved to Minnesota. He became lieutenant governor of that state in 1858 and later served in Congress for eight years. After studying the tales of Atlantis for many years, he brought out in 1882 a vigorous, entertaining book called *Atlantis: The Antediluvian World.* It went through some fifty editions and is still in print. Later Donnelly published other books of a similar nature, as well as a science-fiction novel; and he ran twice for Vice-President of the United States as the candidate of the short-lived Populist Party.

On the first page of *Atlantis: The Antediluvian World,* Donnelly sets forth his basic ideas in this fashion:

"1. That there once existed in the Atlantic Ocean, opposite the mouth of the Mediterranean Sea, a large island, which was the remnant of an Atlantic continent, and known to the ancient world as Atlantis.

"2. That the description of this island given by Plato is not, as has long been supposed, fable, but veritable history.

"3. That Atlantis was the region where man first rose from a state of barbarism to civilization.

"4. That it became, in the course of ages, a populous and mighty nation, from whose overflowings the shores of the Gulf of Mexico, the Mississippi River, the Amazon, the Pacific Coast of South America, the Mediterranean, the west coast of Europe and Africa, the Baltic, the Black Sea, and the Caspian were populated by civilized nations."

There are nine more numbered paragraphs, asserting that the gods and goddesses of the Greeks, Phoenicians, Hindus, and Scandinavians were simply the kings, queens, and heroes of Atlantis; that Atlantis was the actual Garden of

Eden; that Egypt was Atlantis' first colony; that the Atlanteans were the first manufacturers of iron and the inventors of the alphabet; and—

"12. That Atlantis perished in a terrible convulsion of nature, in which the whole island sunk into the ocean, with nearly all its inhabitants.

"13. That a few persons escaped in ships and on rafts, and carried to the nations east and west the tidings of the appalling catastrophe, which has survived to our own time in the Flood and Deluge legends of the different nations of the Old and New worlds."

As Donnelly develops these ideas, he weaves an amazing fabric out of every scrap of myth available to him, from the deluge legends of Mesopotamia to the chronicles of the native kingdoms of Central America. He cites legends of the Toltecs—preserved by the Spanish conquerors of Mexico, who got them from the Aztecs—according to which "the Toltecs traced their migration back to a starting-point called 'Aztlan' or 'Atlan.' This could be no other than Atlantis. . . . The Aztecs also claimed to have come originally from Aztlan. Their very name, Aztecs, was derived from Aztlan. They were Atlanteans." Donnelly observes that "The Western shores of Atlantis were not far distant from the West Indies; a people possessed of ships could readily pass from island to island until they reached the continent. . . . We can therefore readily believe that commercial intercourse between Atlantis and Yucatán, Honduras, and Mexico, created colonies along the shores of the Gulf which gradually spread into the interior, and to the high table-lands of Mexico. And, accordingly, we find that all the traditions of Central America and Mexico point to some country in the East, and beyond the sea, as the source of their first civilized people; and this region, known among them as 'Aztlan,' lived in the memory of the people as a beautiful and happy land, where their ancestors had dwelt in peace for many generations."

To support this theory, Donnelly brings forth a long series of cultural parallels designed to show that every aspect of civilization originated in Atlantis. He asserts that one third of the Mayan language is pure Greek; that the flat-topped pyramids of Mexico are kin to the pointed ones of Egypt; that an Indian language of Mexico is related to Chinese; that Chiapanec, a Central American tongue, resembles Hebrew; and that such cultural traits as the use of spears, sails, metals, and agriculture stem from a common source. Most of these statements, particularly those concerning language, are simply wrong; the others can be accounted for by explanations less complicated than the idea of an ancestral lost continent.

Mound building is one of the cultural traits Donnelly lists. "The mounds of Europe and Asia were made in the same way and for the same purposes as those of America," he declares, offering tales of mound building out of Homer, Herodotus, and other ancient Greek writers; he claims that burial-mound design and structure was the same in Ohio, ancient Britain, and Mesopotamia. Again, some of this is untrue, the rest phrased in such a way that it would make any trait seem to be related to any other. But everything goes into Donnelly's weird, wild theory—including the Davenport elephants:

"We find in America numerous representations of the elephant. We are forced to one of two conclusions: either the monuments date back to the time of the mammoth in North America, or these people held intercourse at some

time in the past with races who possessed the elephant, and
from whom they obtained pictures of that singular animal.
Plato tells us that the Atlanteans possessed great numbers
of elephants." The Wisconsin elephant mound, Donnelly
claims, is "so perfect in its proportions, and complete in its
representation of an elephant, that its builders must have
been well acquainted with all the physical characteristics of
the animal which they delineated." As for the Louisa
County elephant pipe, it is "of the ordinary Mound Builder's
type, and has every appearance of age and usage. There
can be no doubt of its genuineness."

The Mound Builders, according to Donnelly, were off-
shoots of the Atlantean colonies in Mexico. "What would
be more natural," he asks, "than that these adventurous
navigators, passing around the shores of the Gulf, should,
sooner or later, discover the mouth of the Mississippi River;
and what more certain than that they would enter it, explore
it, and plant colonies along its shores, wherever they found a
fertile soil and salubrious climate?" He argues that the
Mound Builders spread up the Mississippi and as far west
as Oregon via the Missouri and Yellowstone rivers.

He praises the complexity of their civilization: their geometrical accuracy, their system of weights and measures,
and so forth. He reports that "the Mound Builders made
sun-dried brick mixed with rushes, as the Egyptians made
sun-dried bricks mixed with straw." (The Mississippi Valley
mounds were made of earth, not of brick.) He declares that
"the Mound Builders also understood the art of casting
metals, or they held intercourse with some race who did,"
and digs up Hildreth's 1819 Marietta find of copper supposedly plated with silver, quoting an opinion by Squier
that the copper was "absolutely *plated*, not simply *overlaid*,

with silver." Donnelly also offers Squier's manatee and toucan pipes as proof of contact between Ohio and the tropics.

He is convinced that the Mound Builders were extremely
ancient. The fact that the mounds had yielded many objects
of copper and none of bronze indicates to him that the
settlers in America had left Atlantis before the discovery of
the art of making bronze. The withdrawal of the Mound
Builders from the territory of the United States and the
migration back into Mexico took place, he thinks, "some
time between A.D. 29 and A.D. 231." He adds, "The hostile
nations which attacked them came from the north; and
when the Mound Builders could no longer hold the country,
or when Atlantis sunk in the sea, they retreated in the direction whence they came, and fell back upon their kindred
races in Central America, as the Roman troops in Gaul and
Britain drew southward upon the destruction of Rome."

Many writers have attempted this kind of speculative
thinking. By drawing together as many supposed resemblances and parallels as possible, and mixing everything up
in a glib and entertaining way, they can "prove" almost any
theory. But few have done it as amusingly and as convincingly as the expert on lost Atlantis, Ignatius T. T. Donnelly.

5

Not everyone was guilty of such misplaced ingenuity.
One voice of reason at the time was Frederic W. Putnam,
curator of Harvard's Peabody Museum. Putnam, born in
1839, came from the same old New England family to
which Rufus Putnam, the founder of Marietta, Ohio, belonged. His original field of interest was birds; while studying at Harvard he became deeply fascinated by fishes; but

by the time he was made head of the Peabody Museum in 1875 he was spending much of his time on archaeology and ethnology. He was a wide-ranging, intelligent, and open-minded man, much respected by his fellow scientists.

Putnam did not accept most of the current myths of the ancient American past. He leaned slightly to the side of those who thought that the Mound Builders were superior to the Indians; describing one group of artifacts taken from the Ohio mounds in 1882, he said, "These relics seem to show a more complex social life, more abundant and varied artistic products, and a higher status altogether, than can be deemed consistent with the views of those who hold that these Mound-builders were merely the ancestors of our present Indians, and in the same state of culture." Considering what we now know about the builders of the Ohio mounds, this statement is entirely correct: they *were* of "a higher status altogether" than the nomadic Indian huntsmen of the nineteenth century. Of course, anyone who said then that he thought the Mound Builders were superior to the Indians of the day would seem to be supporting the mighty-vanished-empire idea, but that was not Putnam's belief at all.

In 1888 he advanced the theory that instead of a single race of Mound Builders there was a succession of mound-building races in the Ohio Valley. He was the first to offer this idea, now universally accepted. Putnam wrote: "In the great Ohio Valley we have found places of contact and mixture of two races, and have made out much of interest, telling of conflict and defeat, of the conquered and the con-querors. The long, narrow-headed people from the north . . . meeting the short-headed southern race, here and there. Our explorations have brought to light considerable evidence to show that . . . a race of men, with short, broad heads, reached the valley from the southwest. Here they cultivated the land, raised crops of corn and vegetables, and became skilled artisans in stone and their native metals, in shell and terra-cotta, making weapons and ornaments and utensils of various kinds. Here were their places of worship. Here were their towns, often surrounded by earth embankments, their fixed places for burning their dead, their altars of clay, where cremation offerings, ornaments, by thousands were thrown upon the fire. Upon the hills near by were their places of refuge or fortified towns. . . ." Before them were other people, going back to those of eight or ten thousand years ago who hunted the mastodon and the mammoth. After them came simpler people, who had no knowledge of the mounds and embankments among which they dwelt.

Putnam also dealt with the controversy over the metal-working skills of the Mound Builders. Ever since Dr. Samuel Hildreth had reported finding objects of copper and silver in the Marietta mounds, the legend of these skills had grown continuously, until many people now believed that the Mound Builders had been able to plate metal upon metal, to cast iron, even to make steel. Putnam was able to explode these theories by going back to the original archaeological reports. The traces of "iron rust" reported by Atwater and others, Putnam said, could actually have been traces of copper rust. If the mound people had used iron at all, which was doubtful, it must have been meteoritic iron found in a natural state and cold-hammered into shape. (Putnam was correct; the mound folk were not capable of refining or casting iron.)

In the case of Hildreth's spool-shaped copper objects, "overlaid with a thick plate of silver," Putnam was able to show that these were ear ornaments; his 1882 mound exca-

vations in Ohio produced a large number of similar artifacts, including one pair next to a skull. "The plating," he
wrote, "has been done simply by covering the outer surfaces of the objects with thin sheets of the overlaid metal,
which were closely united to the copper simply by pounding
and rubbing, and by turning the edges over and under the
slightly concave edge of the copper foundation." These ear-
ornaments "exhibit a degree of skill in working the native
metals of copper, silver and iron, simply by hammering,"
Putnam said. But they provided no reason whatever to think
that the Mound Builders had had any unusual grasp of the
technology of metallurgy. They were clever craftsmen; but
they were not scientists.

17   Copper ear plugs, Lauderdale County, Alabama. Cour-
      tesy Museum of the American Indian, Heye Foundation,
      New York.

6

Cyrus Thomas of the Bureau of Ethnology was now deep
in the mound investigations that Congress had so unexpectedly thrust upon Major Powell's bureau. In 1883 and
1884 the project expanded greatly. Thomas himself remained in Washington most of the time, like a general
directing his troops from the rear lines; he plotted areas of

attack, classified the artifacts that flooded into the Smithsonian, and brooded over the task of studying all of the nation's thousands of mounds.

Ideally, Thomas knew, the way to do things was first to make a detailed survey of all the mounds and excavate them later. But lack of money and manpower, along with other handicaps, made such a survey impossible. Compiling a full set of maps and charts of the mounds, Thomas discovered, would use up the Bureau of Ethnology's whole budget for at least ten years. And during that time the mounds would remain open to the raids of private collectors and the destruction imposed on them by impatient farmers wishing to plow their fields.

So he had to scrap the idea of charting first, digging later. Too many mounds would vanish forever before the mapping was done. Another plan was to pick one particular mound zone and work there until it was fully charted, excavated, and analyzed, and then move on to another zone. But this, too, had drawbacks. It would leave Bureau of Ethnology personnel idle for much of the year, since they would not be able to work in the chosen zone in the winter, and probably their summer work would be thwarted by farmers trying to plant and harvest crops on the land where most mounds were found.

Therefore, Thomas chose a course that left him open to the charge of spreading himself too thin. He decided to carry on operations at a number of places at once, moving his men about to meet seasonal conditions, excavating sites as soon as they were surveyed, without waiting for a broad pattern to emerge from the entire mound district, and leaving one site for another once its immediate value seemed exhausted.

The purpose of the work, Thomas said, was to answer Major Powell's question: "Were the mound builders Indians?" If the answer was yes, "There would then be no more blind groping by archaeologists for the threads to lead them out of the mysterious labyrinth; the chain which binds together the prehistoric and the historic ages of our country would then be known; a thousand and one wild theories and archaeological romances would be relegated to the shades of oblivion. . . ." If the answer was no, it would at least close one vexing debate.

In 1883 and 1884 Thomas had six men at work. P. W. Norris dug in West Virginia during warm weather, in Arkansas during the winter. James D. Middleton spent the summer and fall of 1883 exploring Wisconsin's burial mounds; in the winter he, too, went to Arkansas. L. H. Thing worked in the southeastern counties of Missouri and the northeastern portion of Arkansas. John P. Rogan worked in Florida and Georgia, where he dug at the giant Etowah Mound near Cartersville. Dr. Edward Palmer's zone of operation was Alabama and southwestern Georgia, and John W. Emmert worked in Tennessee and North Carolina.

From their research Thomas distilled the Bureau of Ethnology's first formal report on the mounds. It took up more than a hundred pages in the Fifth Annual Report, published in 1887.

The archaeologists had found nothing to disprove Major Powell's earlier opinions about the builders of the mounds. Though Thomas says again and again that his conclusions are preliminary and that it is too early to know anything for certain, his own position is clear. He opposes the "lost race" theory and says, "whether the 'Indian theory' proves to be correct or not, I wish to obtain for it at least a fair consideration. I believe the latter theory to be the correct one, as the facts so far ascertained appear to point in that direction, but I am not wedded to it; on the contrary, I am willing to follow the facts wherever they lead."

He agrees that the picture of a mighty nation in the great valley of the Mississippi is "fascinating and attractive." He sees the romance in the image of the downfall of this nation under attack by savages, "leaving behind it no evidences of its existence, its glory, power, and extent save these silent forest-covered remains." But he warns that this image, once it has taken possession of the mind, "warps and biases all conclusions."

Thomas divides the mound regions into eight geographical districts, depending on the kind of mounds found in each —flat-topped pyramids, effigy mounds, conical burial mounds, et cetera. He quotes Frederic Putnam's opinion "that more than one of the several American stocks or nations or groups of tribes built mounds. . . . What their connections were is not yet by any means clear, and to say that they all must have been one and the same people seems to be making a statement directly contrary to the facts, which are yearly increasing as the spade and pick in careful hands brings them to light." Thomas notes that the theory of a single great race of Mound Builders, ruling from Dakota to Florida, from New York to Louisiana, "is fast breaking down before the evidence that is produced."

Then he reports on the work his division has done thus far. He describes and charts mounds in Wisconsin, Iowa, Missouri, Ohio, Illinois, and several other states. One of his purposes is to prove that in some parts of the country mound building went on from prehistoric times almost to the pres-

ent. For example, he produces an account of the mound
burial of an Indian chief in Iowa in 1830; the dead chieftain
went to his grave in a military uniform given him by President Jackson.

Like Squier, Thomas believes that the earthworks of
western New York were built by Indians of historic times.
The effigy mounds of Wisconsin, northern Illinois, and
northeastern Iowa, he thinks, "were built by the Indian
tribes found inhabiting that section at the advent of the
whites, or by their ancestors. . . . But the case is somewhat
different in reference to the works of the Ohio district. Although the data here obtained point with satisfactory certainty to the conclusion that Indians were the authors of
these works, it cannot be claimed that all or even the larger
portion of them were built by Indians inhabiting the district
when first visited by the whites, or by their ancestors." In
trying to identify the builders of these mounds, Thomas
revives Heckewelder's old tale of the Tallegewi, suggesting
that these were the people responsible for the famous Ohio
and West Virginia mounds, and that, driven out of their
homeland in some ancient war, they migrated to the Carolinas and became the modern Cherokees.

But a different people, he feels, produced the giant
Etowah Mound of Georgia. In the course of the digging at
Etowah in 1883–84, certain bizarre and striking artifacts of
a previously unknown type had come to light: thin sheets of
copper on which were stamped or engraved strange and
intricate outlined figures. Several plates showed profiles of
human figures with fiercely hooked noses and savage
mouths; the figures had wings and wore complex headdresses, and were shown dangling severed human heads
from their hands. The designs were vigorous and powerful,

18 Copper plate engraving from Etowah Mound, Georgia. From *Report on the Mound Explorations of the Bureau of Ethnology, Twelfth Annual Report.*

sophisticated yet barbaric. They reminded Major Powell of the art of the Aztecs and Mayas, who also went in for winged figures, men with beaked faces, and severed heads. But Cyrus Thomas, studying the Etowah engravings more carefully, found several features unknown to Mexican and Central American art, such as the placement of the wings. "That these plates are not the work of the Indians found inhabiting the southern sections of the United States, or of their direct ancestors, I freely concede," he wrote, but he noted that they did not seem to be the work of Latin-Amer-

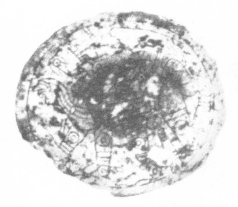

19   Shell disc with incised figure of mythical man-animal,
     Hale County, Alabama. Courtesy of Museum of the
     American Indian, Heye Foundation, New York.

ican artisans either. Thomas was unable to guess at the
identity of the creators of the Etowah plates; he could conclude only that "the Etowah mounds were not built by the
Cherokees."

In a page and a half of summary, Thomas closes this
report—written in 1884—with eight points having to do
with the builders of the mounds. "Different sections were
occupied by different mound-building tribes," he asserts,
"which, though belonging to much the same stage in the
scale of civilization, differed in most instances in habits and
customs. . . ." Nothing about the construction of the mounds
or the artifacts they contained indicated "that their builders
had reached a higher culture-status than that attained by
some of the Indian tribes found occupying the country at the
time of the first arrival of Europeans." He comments that
the custom of erecting mounds over the dead had contin-

ued in some localities well into historic times, and that the oldest of the mounds probably date from the fifth or sixth century A.D., no earlier. Finally, he declares that all the mounds which have been examined thus far appear to be the work of the native Indian tribes of the United States or their ancestors.

7

Cyrus Thomas's next report on his mound work was a twelve-page booklet published by the Bureau of Ethnology late in 1887. In it he says that hundreds of mound groups have been examined and in most cases surveyed and mapped; more than two thousand mounds have been explored, including nearly every type, from the small conical burial mounds of the North to the huge flat-topped pyramids of the South. A full-scale report on this work, amounting to two large-sized volumes of about 500 pages each, is now in preparation, Thomas announces. But he was unable to re- sist mentioning in the booklet "some singular and rather unexpected discoveries":

"From a mound in Wisconsin were obtained a few silver crosses, silver brooches, and silver bracelets, one of the last with the word 'Montreal' stamped on it in plain letters. . . . In another Wisconsin mound, which stands in the midst of a group of effigies, was found, lying at the bottom on the original surface of the ground, near the center, a genuine, regularly-formed gunflint. . . . From a group in Northern Mississippi, in the locality formerly occupied by the Chick- asaw, were obtained a silver plate, with the Spanish coat of arms stamped upon it, and the iron portions of a saddle. . . . In addition to these, the assistants have obtained from mounds such things as brass kettles with iron bails, brass wire, wooden ladles, glass beads, &c." Some of these things had evidently been buried in the mounds long after their original construction, but the position of others showed that they had gone into the mounds when they were being built.

Thomas also declares again that "nothing trustworthy has been discovered to justify the theory that the mound builders belonged to a highly civilized race. . . . The links discovered directly connecting the Indians and mound builders are so numerous and well established that there should be no longer any hesitancy in accepting the theory that the two are one and the same people. . . . Moreover, a study of the works of Ohio and their contents should convince the archaeologist that they were built by several different tribes and pertain to widely different eras." The simple, romantic picture of a Mound Builder empire was coming apart; what Thomas offered in its place was a complex view of many mound-building cultures, difficult to comprehend.

The publication of Thomas' promised major work on the mounds was certain to be an important event in American archaeology. It was awaited with eagerness by some, and with tense, irritable impatience by others who knew it would attack their pet theories. But the immense job of compiling and illustrating the material dragged on and on through the 1880's. Thomas issued a few minor booklets on the mounds in 1889; the great work was still unpublished as the new decade began.

One of the 1889 booklets was called *The Problem of the Ohio Mounds*. This 50-page work repeats Thomas' belief in "an unbroken chain connecting the mound-builders and historical Indians," and dwells in detail on the subject of "the Cherokees as Mound-Builders." Thomas returns to his notion that the Cherokees were Heckewelder's Tallegewi, forced to emigrate from Ohio to the Carolinas, and continuing to build mounds on a lesser scale in their new territory. He quotes William Bartram and others concerning the "town houses" of the Cherokees—large community buildings placed atop artificial mounds—in order to show that the present mounds of Tennessee and the Carolinas are the remains of these sites, which had been built as late as the eighteenth century. He brings forth many arguments to support this idea; but none of them are accepted today. The earthworks of Ohio bear little resemblance to those of Tennessee and the Carolinas. In his zeal to wipe out the lost-race theory, Thomas was often too eager to look upon recent Indian tribes as the builders of the great enclosures and embankments.

The second 1889 bulletin was entitled *The Circular, Square, and Octagonal Earthworks of Ohio.* It tells how Thomas set out to disprove one of Squier's chief points: that the extraordinary geometrical talents of the Mound Builders shows the advanced state of their civilization.

He was skeptical of the measurements of the Ohio mounds provided by Squier and Davis, since their figures were given in round numbers and did not include precise information about how the mounds were surveyed. He speaks of "an inexcusable degree of carelessness, which . . . to a great extent destroys confidence in their measurements and figures." So Thomas sent surveyors of his own to go over the same structures with the proper instruments. The surveyors corrected many errors made by Squier and Davis; but to Thomas's surprise, the findings *still* showed that the Ohio enclosures were geometrically perfect. The "somewhat unexpected results," as Thomas calls them, indicated that

several circular enclosures were laid out as flawlessly as
though surveyors' instruments had been used, while the
angles of the square and octagonal enclosures were mathe-
matically correct.

"The first question which presents itself in view of these
facts," says a somewhat embarrassed Cyrus Thomas, "is,
How are we to reconcile them with the theory that the
works were built by Indians?" He can offer no real answer
—except to say that the Indians who built them must have
had some very clever methods of designing huge enclosures.

                                    8

Each new annual report of the Bureau of Ethnology promised that Thomas' huge manuscript on the mounds would
soon see print. But Thomas continued to revise and rear-
range his work, now and then making a journey to some
distant site to check on a doubtful point. To archaeologists
of the day, Thomas' ever-growing manuscript was taking
on legendary characteristics of its own. But the Eleventh
Annual Report, published in 1894, revealed that it would
shortly be published; and the Twelfth Annual Report, published later that same year, devoted all of its 730 pages to
Thomas' monumental paper, "Report on the Mound Explorations of the Bureau of Ethnology."

This was the third of the three great works on the mounds
written in the nineteenth century. It dwarfed the earlier
efforts of Atwater and of Squier and Davis both in bulk and
in breadth of approach. It was also the last such general
account that could ever be assembled since—largely due to
Thomas—the whole concept of a single "Mound Builder"
culture would now have to be scrapped, and future surveys

would have to deal with many different cultures that had indulged in building mounds.

The report was not intended for laymen, and little of it makes lively reading. Its main section, nearly 500 pages, is simply a digest of field research, describing thousands of mounds all over the country. Before and after this mass of material, though, Thomas offers his interpretations and speculations.

In a brief foreword he states once more his belief that the Mound Builders and the Indians belong to one race. Though this was correct, he failed to see that there were gaps of hundreds or even thousands of years, in some cases, between the building of certain mound groups and the arrival in those areas of the Indians of historic times. Thus his "apparently conclusive" proof that the Cherokees had built most of the Tennessee and North Carolina mounds turned out to be not so conclusive, nor do today's archaeologists accept his argument that the Cherokees had created most of the West Virginia mounds and "some of the principal works of Ohio." But these were forgivable errors; Thomas' effort to deflate the myth led him to go too far in the opposite direction, away from lost-race fantasies. No one today can quarrel with his main conclusion: "Although much the larger portion of the ancient monuments of our country belong to prehistoric times, and some of them, possibly, to the distant past, yet the evidence of contact with European civilization is found in so many mounds . . . that it must be conceded that many of them were built subsequent to the discovery of the continent by Europeans."

The immense catalog of mound descriptions that takes up the heart of the report is dry and detailed. ("No. 22. Sixty feet in diameter and 5 feet high. First foot, soil; the

rest black, mucky earth, with a slight admixture of sand. At
the depth of 2 feet were seven skeletons, with heads in
various directions, some stretched out with the faces up,
others folded, also other bones. At the center, about 3 feet
down, were a few rib bones, apparently the remains of a
skeleton, over which lay a copper plate. . . .") The descriptions are accompanied by diagrams, charts, and illustrations
of artifacts. Nearly all of the mounds discussed by Thomas
have since been destroyed, except a few preserved in public
parks, and so modern archaeologists must rely on Thomas'
published accounts for their entire knowledge of most of
these sites.

The long series of excavation reports is followed by an
essay of some 80 pages on the types and distribution of
mounds. It shows with great force and skill why it is impossible to credit all the earthworks to a single "race." Lastly,
under the heading, "General Observations," Thomas reviews
the entire mound problem as it had unfolded since the eighteenth century, dealing in turn with each of the theories he
has overthrown.

He quotes from many well-known writers on the mounds
such phrases as "an ancient race entirely distinct from the
Indians," "a nation with a central administration," and "a
knowledge of art and methodical labor foreign to the red
man." Calmly, coolly, he deflates the lost-race myth, arguing
that the mounds are of such widely differing types that they
could not possibly all have been built by the same culture.

Thomas quarrels with the "evidence" offered to show how
ancient the mounds are. One point, stressed by Atwater and
also by Squier and Davis, is that few of the mounds of Ohio
are found on the most recent of the terraces of earth formed
by rivers as they cut through the soil. This was supposed to

show that the latest of the terraces had been formed after the mounds were built. Thomas merely points out that such terraces were more subject to floods than the other terraces higher up, which was sufficient reason for not building anything on them.

The size of the earthworks had been used as an argument to prove that they must have been built by a race that had better tools and a more tightly organized government than any Indian tribe. But Thomas shows that Indians of quite recent times were able to organize governments and to carry out extensive building projects. And if the Mound Builders had superior tools, where have they gone? "It is true that when we stand at the base of the great Cahokia mound [in Illinois] and study its vast proportions, we can scarcely bring ourselves to believe it was built without some other means of collecting and conveying material than that possessed by the Indians," he wrote. "But what other means could a lost race have had? The Indians had wooden spades, baskets, skins of animals, wooden and clay vessels, and textile fabrics; they also had stone implements. Moreover, the fact should be borne in mind that this great mound is unique in respect to size, being more than treble in contents that of any other true mound in the United States. . . . As a general rule the labor necessary to build them could not have exceeded that which has often been performed by Indians. It is also more than likely that all the people of a tribe, both men and women, aided in the work, and that the large works were built by additions made during successive generations."

What of the inscribed tablets found in certain mounds? Are these not proof of a non-Indian origin? Thomas has some fun with the various translators of the Grave Creek Tablet; he maintains that the inscriptions on such tablets were purely decorative, not words or letters at all. He looks also at the Davenport tablets and pipes, and uses his own experience as a field archaeologist to show that the Iowans' own reported details indicate the tablets must have been planted by pranksters. Generously, he expresses his belief that Jacob Gass and the other members of the Davenport Academy of Natural Sciences were innocent victims of the hoax.

"Another objection to the theory that the mound-builders were Indians," Thomas goes on, "is based on the oft-repeated statement of the Indians that they know nothing of the origin of these works; that when they first entered the territory they found them already built and abandoned." A good point, but he has a good answer: "These same Indians have not the faintest tradition of some of the most important events in their own history dating back less than two centuries. For example, de Soto's expedition, although it must have been the most remarkable event in the past history of the southern tribes, seems to have been forgotten by them when the French adventurers, 130 years later, appeared on the scene." He uses the narratives of de Soto's chroniclers to show that mounds were still being built in the South in the sixteenth century; he identifies some of the actual mounds mentioned by the chroniclers. With some amusement, Thomas comments that these eyewitness accounts by Europeans were forgotten within a century, so that the southern mounds were rediscovered "one by one, and are looked upon by the new generation which has arisen, as strange and mysterious mementos of a 'long lost' and 'unknown' race. . . . Is it strange that the 'untutored savage,' without writings or records, should in a few—a very few— generations lose sight of the past when our own civilized race forgets in the same time?"

At the end, briefly, Thomas considers the theory that the Mound Builders came from Mexico or Central America. He finds no evidence for a migration from the tropics, however, and regards most of the supposed examples of contact between Mexico and the mound region as exaggerated. But his discussion of this point, coming after more than 700 pages of evidence have been presented, shows signs of fatigue; his ideas are sketchily outlined.

The work as a whole, however, is impressive. It represents a formidable gathering of data and a generally sensible evaluation of it. He had thoroughly and convincingly shown that the mounds were the work of a number of different cultures, none of them outside the great family of American Indian tribes.

Cyrus Thomas's great report marked the end of an era. No longer could one speak of "the Mound Builders" in quite the same way, as masters of a vast empire. But Thomas had raised as many questions as he had answered. His work was not so much an epilogue as a prologue. It still was necessary for archaeologists to examine the contents of the mounds more closely, to analyze the cultural traits of their builders, to discover relationships and differences—in short, to develop a clear picture of the prehistoric American past.

▲▲▲ 6

THE HONORED DEAD:
ADENA AND HOPEWELL

▲▲▲

One of the important points Cyrus Thomas raised is that before we can ask ourselves whether it was Indians or Mound Builders who built the mounds, we must know the answer to the question, "What is an Indian?" The standard nineteenth-century response was to point to the nomadic horsemen of the Western plains—the hard-riding "Injuns" familiar to all of us from too many motion pictures. But that was too simple. Also belonging in the class, "Indian," were such peoples as the totem-pole builders of the Pacific Northwest, the pueblo-dwellers of Arizona and New Mexico, the farmers who once had inhabited the Southeast, the forest huntsmen of the North, and many more. There were hundreds of totally unrelated Indian languages, and thousands of tribal units. Some Indians were plump, others lean; some round-headed, others long-headed; some hawk-nosed, some flat-nosed. Though there were certain traits that all people called "Indians" held in common, the term was actually so vague that it defined very little other than the natives of the Americas in general. In that case, Thomas asked, why set up high boundaries between the class of "Indians" and the class of "Mound Builders"? Why not accept the fact that the various mound-building tribes had simply been Indians of a high culture and social organization?

Against the background of Thomas's common-sense arguments, other men groped toward a solution of the problem of the Mound Builders. They went looking in the mounds for answers, excavating in a sober, methodical way, letting the evidence they uncovered shape their theories instead of starting with theories and trying to make the evidence fit. They were not out to "prove" anything. They were willing to wait until all the facts had been gathered before drawing conclusions.

William C. Mills of the Ohio State Museum published his report on Ohio's Adena Mound in 1902, on the Edwin Harness Mound in 1907, on the Seip Mound in 1909. Clarence B. Moore of Philadelphia explored the mounds of Florida from 1892 to 1903, and spent the years from 1905 to 1913 searching for mounds along the rivers of Arkansas, Louisiana, Mississippi, and Alabama. Warren K. Moorehead of Ohio wrote on Fort Ancient in 1890, and began his excavation of the important Hopewell Group the following year. Harvard's Peabody Museum sponsored a number of Ohio expeditions under F. W. Putnam. There were many more such pioneers. Their reports were published mainly in technical journals. The general public went on thinking of a mysterious lost race, the Mound Builders, but archaeologists now referred to "the so-called Mound Builders" or to "the supposed Mound Builders." The concept of the Mound Builders had perished, but for the moment there was nothing to put in its place.

The situation was still confused when Roland B. Dixon,

president of the American Anthropological Association, spoke to that organization in December 1913 on current problems of archaeology. In discussing the Ohio Valley he remarked, "The history of this region is a more than ordinarily complicated one, and . . . we must admit here the presence of the remains of a number of different cultures." He called the puzzle of the mounds "one of rather baffling complexity. A satisfactory classification even of the various types present is by no means easy." The tone of these comments is quite different from that of the nineteenth century. Instead of the confident evaluations of men like Squier, Dixon offers hesitant, tentative, doubt-filled statements.

Through much of the first half of the twentieth century, American archaeologists wrestled with problems of understanding and classifying. There were fierce professional debates over terms and concepts. Some of the debates are still going on. The problem was to turn prehistory into history by creating a system of eras and periods that would bring order out of misty confusion. Today such a system exists. It is still somewhat tentative, still undergoing minor revisions; it is still subject even to major reconsideration in the light of new evidence. But as it stands it provides a means of finding one's way around in the patterns of prehistoric events in the United States, both in the regions where mounds are found and outside them.

2

The most recent attempt at creating such a system—and the one that many archaeologists today prefer—is the one set forth by Gordon R. Willey of Harvard University in

1966 in *An Introduction to American Archaeology,* which makes use of a system depending on the distinction between cultural *traditions* and chronological *periods.*

For Willey and other archaeologists, a *culture* is a specific social group with a distinct way of life. For instance, the Adena Culture of Ohio and surrounding states was typified by the building of conical burial mounds and by such other identifiying traits as the use of copper, the habit of employing hard cradleboards to flatten babies' skulls for decorative purposes, and particular shapes of beads and pipes.

The Adena Culture is considered an example of the Early Woodland Tradition. A *tradition,* in this system, is a broadly defined way of life, practiced in more or less the same manner by different cultures at different times. There was only one Adena Culture, but the Woodland Tradition can be traced in nearly all parts of the country as far west as the Great Plains. The chief features of the Woodland Tradition were the beginnings of agriculture, the manufacture of pottery, and the development of permanent village settlements. These are all features of a cultural stage, not of a specific time period. East of the Mississippi, many Indian groups began to reach this cultural stage as early as 1000 B.C., but farther west another thousand years or more passed before the group of concepts making up the Woodland Tradition took hold.

A *period* is a certain span of time during which a particular tradition is dominant. In Ohio, where the Woodland Tradition was the main way of life from about 1000 B.C. to A.D. 700, the term *Burial Mound Period* has been assigned to those centuries. This is a method of measuring time; we can speak of events taking place during a certain

period, but not during a certain tradition. The Burial
Mound Period refers to the years when the Woodland
Tradition happened to be dominant in Ohio.

Willey lists four traditions in eastern North America:
Big-Game Hunting, Archaic, Woodland, and Mississippian.

20   A Chronological Chart of the Prehistory of Eastern
     North America (after Gordon R. Willey).

Approximate dates	Period	Tradition	Characteristics of Tradition
20,000(?)– 8,000 B.C. (Glacial Era)	Paleo-Indian Early Middle Late	Big-game Hunting Early Middle Late	Nomadic hunting cultures; stone weapons, knowledge of fire.
7,000– 1,000 B.C.	Archaic Early Middle Late	Archaic Early Middle Late	More or less permanent village life; with some seasonal travel; improved weapons, greater reliance on fishing and food-gathering.
1,000 B.C.– 700 A.D.	Burial Mound I Burial Mound II	Woodland Early Middle Late	Farming cultures with expanded population and more complex social structure; use of pottery; burial mounds.
700 A.D.– 1700 A.D.	Temple Mound I Temple Mound II	Mississippian Early Middle Late	Stockaded towns and agricultural life; fine pottery and art work; temple mound structures.

A *period* is a fixed span of time during which a given tradition was dominant; a *tradition* is a broadly defined way of life practiced in more or less the same way by different cultures at different times.

A *culture* is a specific social group with a distinct way of life. The Hopewell and Adena cultures existed during the Burial Mound Period and were representative of Woodland Tradition; many specific cultures—Tchefuncte, Poverty Point, Dalton, etc.—existed in the Mississippi Valley and southeastern United States during the Temple Mound Period and exhibited the characteristics of the Mississippian Tradition.

These arrived in different sections at different times; it was quite possible for one area to be inhabited by tribes living in the Woodland Tradition while backward tribes nearby still maintained the way of life of the Archaic Tradition.

In the same geographical area Willey lists four major periods, each pegged to a particular time span by the most reliable data available. These are the Paleo-Indian, Archaic, Burial Mound, and Temple Mound periods. (The Archaic *Tradition*—a cluster of cultural traits—should not be confused with the Archaic *Period*—the era from 7000 to 1000 B.C.)

The four traditions are subdivided into Early, Middle, and Late phases. The four periods are also divided; Willey speaks of Early, Middle, and Late Archaic periods, Burial Mound I and II, Temple Mound I and II. Within this structure there are local series of cultures. In Louisiana, the Early Archaic Period was the time of the Dalton Culture; the Late Archaic was the time of the Poverty Point Culture; Burial Mound I the time of the Tchefuncte Culture; and so on through Temple Mound II. In other regions there are different local cultures representing the sequence of traditions from Archaic through Woodland to Mississippian. They all fit into the same broad cultural pattern, but have their own special traits.

Man reached the New World very late in his evolutionary career. Paleontologists have uncovered many human fossils quite different in physical form from modern man—such as Neanderthal man or Java's *Pithecanthropus erectus*. Some of the fossil human types found in Africa lived nearly two million years ago. From this fossil evidence scientists conclude that man went through a series of evolutionary changes before taking on approximately his present appearance less than 100,000 years ago.

But there were no human beings at all in the Western Hemisphere during this evolutionary period. At least, no fossils of really primitive human forms have ever been discovered here. So far as the fossil record shows, the whole story of human evolution took place overseas, and when man got to the Americas he was already in his modern form.

His migration route lay via the Bering Strait out of Asia into Alaska, and down into North America. Those who believed in the myth of the Mound Builders tended to think that he had arrived a long time ago—10,000, 20,000, even 100,000 years ago. After the myth was exploded, many conservative scientists—particularly those of the Smithsonian Institution—insisted that the first men had arrived in the New World within the last three or four thousand years. There followed a fierce scientific battle, which did not end until 1927, when an archaeologist digging near Folsom, New Mexico, unearthed the skeleton of a kind of bison that scientists agreed had been extinct for eight to ten thousand years. Between the bison's ribs was a stone weapon point. The Folsom discovery showed that man had lived in the New World at the time when such great woolly beasts as the bison and the mammoth still roamed. On the basis of this and later evidence, including the results of the radioactive-testing process known as carbon-14 dating, it is now thought that men first reached the New World between 15,000 and 40,000 years ago.

These people are known as Paleo-Indians ("ancient Indians") and their culture is called the Big-Game Hunting Tradition. The time in which they flourished—down to about 8000 B.C.—is termed the Paleo-Indian Period.

The Paleo-Indians lived at a time when the climate of the United States was colder and more rainy than it is today. Huge animals which are now extinct lived here—the ground sloth, the great bison, the mammoth, and others. The Paleo-Indians hunted them. They knew nothing of farming and had no villages; and of course they built no mounds or earthworks. They wandered from place to place, following the big game that was their chief food supply.

About 8000 B.C. North America grew warmer and drier, and as the climate changed the big animals slowly began to die out. Man found himself forced to make great adjustments in his way of life. The Big-Game Hunting Tradition gave way to the Archaic Tradition.

This new way of life seems to have arisen first in the woodlands of the East before 5000 B.C., possibly as early as 7000 or 8000 B.C. It spread slowly westward. Some regions continued to practice the Big-Game Hunting Tradition long after others had moved into the Archaic Tradition.

The characteristics of the Archaic Tradition are improved weapons, greater reliance on fishing and plant-gathering, and the founding of semi-permanent villages. Archaic peoples learned how to stalk animals in the forest and how to strike them down with barbed or notched points. They made handsome chopping and scraping tools of polished stone, and discovered how certain seeds could be milled with grinding stones to make them edible. They were not mound builders. Since Archaic Indians did not cultivate their own food or keep domestic animals, they had to travel with the seasons, moving in regular patterns to stay near their sources of fish and shellfish, meats, berries, and roots. But they usually returned regularly to the village that was their home base.

While the relatively simple Archaic Tradition was dominant here, the Indians of Mexico and South America were mastering agriculture and pottery, and their cultures rapidly grew more complex. Farming was more efficient than food-gathering and allowed the community leisure to develop social and spiritual concepts, as well as technical ideas. Some of the advanced ideas of the south began filtering into the United States between 1000 B.C. and the time of Christ, causing another cultural shift.

In the Southwest, the development of agriculture and pottery led toward the flowering of the Pueblo culture. In the East and on the prairies, the Woodland Tradition developed. It was marked by an expanding population, a change-over to farming, the making of pottery, and, apparently, a new religion. Archaic peoples had been content with simple burials, but the Woodland Tradition folk devoted much effort to building tombs for their dead. This trait is noted in the name given to the period that began in the East about 1000 B.C.—Burial Mound I. As the Archaic Tradition gave way to the Woodland Tradition, the Archaic Period came to its end and the Burial Mound Period began.

3

Archaeologists are now fairly sure who the first mound builders of North America were. These earthworks pioneers are known as the Adena people, and their existence as a culture has been recognized since the beginning of this century.

The culture takes its name from Adena, the Chillicothe, Ohio, estate of Thomas Worthington, who was governor of Ohio from 1814 to 1818. In 1901, William C. Mills, cu-

21 The Adena pipe. Courtesy Ohio Historical Society, Columbus, Ohio.

rator of the Ohio State Archaeological and Historical Society, excavated a great mound on the grounds of Adena and found within it log tombs, objects of mica, copper bracelets, and other distinctive artifacts—including the famous Adena Pipe, a yellow and red clay figure of a stocky, perhaps dwarfed man.

Mills regarded the artifacts found in the Adena Mound as different enough from those discovered in most other Ohio mounds to warrant coining a distinct Adena Culture name —this at a time when the practice of using such local names had barely come into use. He included in Adena certain other previously excavated mounds, such as the Grave Creek Mound in West Virginia and the big Miamisburg Mound in Ohio. The special Adena traits he listed included conical burial mounds; uncremated burials in log tombs;

the use of copper and mica; and the use of tube-shaped tobacco pipes.

For a long time Adena's place within the prehistoric pattern remained uncertain. The first detailed study of the culture appeared in 1932 in the *Ohio State Archaeological and Historical Quarterly,* which had published many of the basic reports on Ohio mounds. Its author, Emerson F. Greenman, identified 70 mounds as being of the Adena type and noted 59 cultural traits found in these mounds. Greenman's work was hampered by the poor condition of the mounds; many of them had been ruined by artifact-hunting local citizens, and even those that had been opened by nineteenth-century archaeologists were in bad shape.

In the 1930's the Federal Government undertook an extensive program of archaeology under the Works Progress Administration, a plan for keeping people employed during the Depression. A great many mounds were excavated, particularly in Southern states where the new reservoirs of the Tennessee Valley Authority would soon flood archaeological sites; some work was also done in the Ohio mound region. One of the leaders of this enormous government-sponsored enterprise was William S. Webb of the University of Kentucky. In the course of the work, a number of Adena mounds were excavated for the first time, and some of the others were re-excavated. In 1945, Webb and his University of Kentucky colleague Charles E. Snow published a report on the new findings called *The Adena People,* which added 103 Adena sites to Greenman's 70, and expanded his list of 59 cultural traits to 218. By then it was recognized that the Adena folk occupied a significant place in Ohio Valley prehistory. Webb and Snow wrote:

"The point of origin of Adena man with his mound-building traits cannot yet be demonstrated, but it is certain that he was the *first builder of earthworks* in this region, and thus could not have derived these traits from any earlier occupant of the region." They suspected that the Adena people might have come from the South, and perhaps had acquired the mound-building idea from Mexico or Central America.

It was estimated that the Adena Culture had taken form about 1000 B.C. A great concern for the welfare of the dead, marked by the construction of huge earthen tombs, was its key trait. About 400 B.C., archaeologists believed, a new group began to enter the territory of the Adena folk. The newcomers belonged to the Hopewell Culture, named for a site in Ross County, Ohio, where their typical traits were first observed. Skeletal evidence showed that the Hopewells had long, narrow skulls, while the Adenas generally had round, broad skulls. Thus the change in culture was the result of the arrival of a different stock, not merely of the passage of time.

The Hopewells—who really were the "Mound Builders" of whom nineteenth-century writers had made so much—adopted the basic pattern of Adena life, but expanded and transformed it. As Webb and Snow outlined it, the Adenas and the intruding Hopewells lived as uneasy neighbors for hundreds of years, with the Hopewells borrowing most of the Adena traits and carrying them further. They built vast burial mounds and the celebrated earthen embankments covering hundreds of acres. By A.D. 500, the Hopewell Culture had reached its climax in a kind of empire with trade links reaching across much of North America; then it began to fade, and shortly the older Adena Culture joined it in oblivion.

The report of Webb and Snow indicated that many details of the relationship of Adena to its successor, the dynamic Hopewell Culture, were still unknown. In the years that followed there was considerable research on the problems presented by the Adena Culture. One of the leaders in this work was Raymond S. Baby of the Ohio State Museum, who excavated several important Adena mounds in Ohio. Baby's work was largely salvage archaeology: he attempted to rescue what information he could from mounds that were about to be destroyed, and in some cases dug in mounds whose demolition was already under way. With much of the mound region of the United States undergoing great industrial expansion after World War II, virtually every mound not already protected by government ownership was in danger. Archaeologists were compelled to organize their work-schedules according to the plans of the bulldozer men; mounds in no risk of immediate destruction were left unexplored while archaeologists concentrated on salvaging the contents of the threatened ones.

This postwar work was so fruitful that a new compilation of Adena research was needed by 1957. William S. Webb's *The Adena People No. 2,* written in collaboration with Raymond S. Baby and including chapters by other Adena authorities, raised the number of known Adena mounds from 173 to 222, and added 23 new traits to the previous 218. A special feature of the book was its discussion of the dates of the mounds as determined by the carbon-14 process, which had come into use by archaeologists only a few years before. The age of the earliest Adena mound, obtained from charcoal found in the Toepfner Mound in Ohio, was 2780 years, with a possible error of 410 years in either direction. The latest Adena site, according to carbon-14, was the Drake Mound in Kentucky, which registered an age of 1168 years with a possible error of 150 years. These figures gave a range for Adena from about 800 B.C. to A.D. 900. Five samples taken from Hopewell mounds indicated a range of from 600 B.C. to A.D. 1500.

Some of these dates were challenged. They seemed to show that the Adena Culture had lasted for 1700 years and the Hopewell Culture for 2100. The most recent dates were severely questioned, and further examination was demanded. New tests left the early range more or less unchanged, showing the start of Adena between 1000 and 800 B.C. and of Hopewell about 400 B.C. But a second reading for the Drake Mound sample showed that it was about a thousand years older than had previously been thought. Similarly, the most recent Hopewell dates now proved to be about A.D. 500, except for one questionable date of A.D. 900. From the revised carbon-14 evidence, then, it appears that these two mound-building cultures of the Ohio Valley flourished for about fifteen centuries, overlapping during most of that time, and that both were fading out by the fifth century A.D.

One of the most important recent studies of the Adena Culture, published in 1963, challenges many of the earlier conclusions about Adena, and offers some new ideas that many archaeologists are coming to accept. It is *Mounds for the Dead,* by Don W. Dragoo of Pittsburgh's Carnegie Museum, and it is based chiefly on Dragoo's excavation of the Cresap Mound in West Virginia.

This was a salvage archaeology job. In 1958 the Cresap Mound came into the possession of a coal company that intended to build an industrial plant on the site. Archae-

ologists persuaded the company to permit a single excavation
before the mound was destroyed. The company went further
and agreed to supply four full-time workers, some part-time
men, and heavy earth-moving machinery. Under the direction of Dragoo and a team from the Carnegie Museum,
excavation of the mound began on June 2, 1958, and was
finished on August 26.

The mound was a cone 15 feet high and 70 feet in
diameter. Atop it was a locust tree 22 inches thick at the
base, difficult to remove and with roots that spread through
the entire mound, plaguing the archaeologists throughout
their work.

Once the mound surface had been cleared, Dragoo cut
a trial trench that showed him where the base level of the
mound lay; then he began to dig inward from the outside
of the mound. Layers of earth about an inch thick were
cut away by a hoe and shoveled into heaps to be removed
by power equipment. As the earth was gradually stripped
away, an unexpectedly intricate structure was revealed.
Dragoo saw that the Cresap Mound's many layers covered
a vast span in the development of the Adena Culture. "I
was at last presented with the previously missing key to
Adena chronology," he wrote. "Scraps of information that
meant little before now took on new meaning."

The mound had apparently been built on the site of an
early dwelling. Its circular clay floor, about 40 feet in
diameter and several inches thick, rested directly on the
original loose gravel subsoil of the site. At some point long
ago a burial had taken place in the house; a shallow tomb
had been dug in the clay floor, and two bodies were placed
in it. Dark humus-laden soil was heaped over them. Addi-

tional burials followed until a small mound, about five feet high, was formed.

About midway in the growth of this mound, a second tomb was dug in the clay floor, and dark earth was piled over it also. Later, six individuals were buried about 15 feet south of the center of the house site, forming another mound about 3 feet high. A similar mound, slightly more than 5 feet high, was later built over a tomb on the east side of the house. This mound grew in stages, and eight bodies were enclosed in it.

Apparently this entire group of little mounds was covered by a wooden canopy, whose onetime existence is indicated by small particles of charcoal on the surface of the mounds. This covering evidently was destroyed by fire. Next, the entire site was covered with earth, forming a single conical mound 6.75 feet high at its peak. This was allowed to stand for some time; humus accumulated atop it to a depth of several inches, and rain caused erosion gullies to develop.

Later, ceremonial objects were deposited on the mound in the course of further burials, and the overall height reached 8.2 feet. Then a pit was scooped out of the summit and a cremation burial took place in it; 15 small copper beads and a few other artifacts accompanied the tribesman to his rest, and logs were placed above the burial. A cap of earth was added, bringing the height of the mound to 13.25 feet; then the mound was left undisturbed long enough for a 6-inch-thick layer of humus to collect.

Eventually the mound again was used for burial. Another fireplace was constructed at the top, and eight bodies were arranged around it; over these burials and the fireplace a thick cap of gravelly earth was added until the mound reached a height of about 17 feet. Over the centuries erosion removed about two feet of this before the archaeologists arrived.

"With the addition of the above earth mantle," Dragoo wrote, "the building of the Cresap Mound by the Adena people drew to a close. The mound appears not to have been disturbed again until the Late Prehistoric (A.D. 1200–1600) when a man of that period was buried in a shallow pit dug into the top of the mound. Neither this intrusion nor two shallow probings of the mound during the past century caused any disturbance or damage to the mound's structure or contents. To us was presented the rare opportunity of excavating a basically undisturbed mound in which a clear chronological sequence of events could be traced."

The artifacts from the mound included scrapers, drills, blades, and weapon points, along with 370 copper beads, cups and awls of bone, shell beads, 4 pipes, and 22 tablets, one of them an unusual turtle effigy. The tablets, which had no engraved inscriptions, were discovered at all levels of the mound, with the finest near the top. The Cresap Mound is the only one that shows the whole sequence of Adena culture from early to late. From the evidence it contained, Dragoo was able to reconstruct Adena development to give a view quite different from that previously imagined.

4

The picture of Adena life that has emerged from recent research shows a culture concentrated in a circle 300 miles in diameter, with its center at Chillicothe, Ohio. There were two main Adena population centers, one along the Scioto River in southern Ohio and one on the Kanawha River near

Charleston, West Virginia. Minor centers were located in eastern Indiana, northern Kentucky, western Ohio, and northwestern West Virginia. The most easterly of these lesser centers was at Moundsville, West Virginia, surrounding the Grave Creek Mound.

From the heart of the Adena territory, it is possible to trace Adena influence up the Ohio River to Pittsburgh, where a large Adena mound once existed. The presence of Adena ideas has been detected on the eastern shore of Chesapeake Bay, though no mounds were built there, and

22   Map of Adena sites.

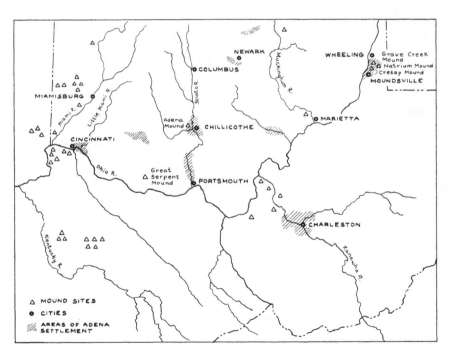

as far south as northern Alabama. Adena traits in New York
State were also reported in 1937 by William A. Ritchie of
the New York State Museum. Only one group of Adena
mounds is known in New York, on Long Sault Island in the
St. Lawrence River. According to Ritchie, who believes that
the site marks the arrival of a band of late-period refugees
from the main Adena territory in Ohio, this is "the outpost
most remote of any now known from the Adena heartland."

The largest and most famous of the Adena sites is the
Grave Creek Mound, entered by its owners in 1838 and
later badly damaged by erosion; today it is an important
tourist attraction, and steps have been taken to preserve it.
Delf Narona conducted the first modern excavations there
in 1957. Don Dragoo considers the Grave Creek Mound
representative of late Adena life.

Dragoo has classified the several hundred known Adena
traits into early, middle, and late styles, and his classification does not always agree with the system used by Webb
and others. Early and middle Adena life, Dragoo says, were
typified by burial of the dead in conical mounds that occurred singly or in groups. Most bodies were simply stretched
out on bark on the surface of the ground; a few were placed
in shallow pits lined with clay and covered with logs. In
this period, Adena houses were circular, made of posts arranged one-deep and lashed together. Adena tools were of
flint or bone; ornaments included copper beads, stone pendants, and headdresses made from deer or elk skulls with
antlers. Sometimes the antlers were imitated in copper.

The coming of the late Adena period was marked by the
custom of burial in elaborate log tombs covered by conical
mounds constructed in groups; frequently a circular earthwork was nearby. These "sacred circles," found in many

parts of the Adena territory, are different from the much larger enclosures of the Hopewell people; none is more than 500 feet in diameter. Other typical late Adena traits are finely made stone tablets, tube-shaped pipes, the use of mica, and a new style of house construction; Adena houses now were walled by double rings of posts. The circular dwellings ranged from 35 to 52 feet in diameter. Larger buildings of similar style apparently served as community centers.

Each village consisted of from two to five houses, each perhaps containing a family group. Clusters of these small villages were distributed over a wide area. Most archaeologists believe that the Adena people were farmers, since a culture devoted to such extensive construction projects would need a steady and reliable food supply. This was confirmed in 1938 when fragments of pumpkin and squash were recovered from the fireplace of the Florence Mound, Pickaway County, Ohio. Carbon-14 dating of this material gave an age of 1425 ± 250 years. Pumpkin rind was later found at another Adena site, the Cowan Mound in Clinton County, Ohio. These are the only traces of Adena agriculture that have come to light so far. Corn, the basic crop of most American Indian farming cultures, is totally absent.

Don Dragoo, unlike most of his colleagues, does not think the Adena people necessarily did much farming. The lack of corn and the presence of cultivated pumpkin and squash at only a couple of late Adena sites led him to think "that early Adena need not have been geared to an agricultural economy . . . in order to have constructed mounds for the burial of the dead. The gradual build-up of a mound, for example the Cresap Mound, did not necessitate the expenditure of great amounts of labor at any one time. By the use of every source of food that was available from hunting, and gathering of wild plants, early Adena could easily have established the scattered pattern of settlement that marks the culture. . . . If agriculture, and specifically cultivation of corn, did become an important factor in Adena, I feel that it must have been very late." Whether or not the Adena folk were farmers, they depended heavily on such wild plants as raspberry, chestnut, pawpaw, and walnut; they also collected snails and fresh-water mussels, and hunted deer, elk, black bear, raccoon, beaver, and many other animals.

The central fact of Adena life was the cult of the honored dead. This began simply, with low mounds over burial pits as found in the core of the Cresap Mound, and gradually became more elaborate. At the outset some of the dead were buried, others cremated, some left on exposed platforms until the flesh was gone and the bundled bones alone could be interred. Some experts think that only important leaders received tomb burials and that ordinary men were cremated; but Dragoo observes that valuable objects often were burned along with bodies, while some of the tomb burials do not yield such goods. We still do not know why there were so many types of early Adena burials, but there can be no doubt that the ritual act of burial—with its implied belief in an afterlife—was very important to the Adena folk even at the beginning of their development.

The objects left beside the bodies in the burial mounds tell us a great deal about Adena craftsmanship. Mostly they were such things as pottery, blades, drills, awls, and scrapers —perhaps the property of the person with whom they were buried. Usually a single pipe was placed with each burial, although in one mound 32 pipes were arranged about one body. "Why?" Dragoo wonders. "Was this man the pipe-maker? Was this a way of paying tribute to a revered individual in which the men of clan gave up their prized pipes? Was the pipe of special significance in their ceremonies? If so, why were pipes placed with some persons and not with others? Did only certain individuals have the rights to a pipe? These and many other questions goad the archaeologist. . . ."

The late Adena period, which saw so many sweeping changes in Adena customs, apparently produced a deepening and enrichment of the burial cult. This period has yielded a harvest of superb Adena art. Now, it seems, only a few privileged individuals were buried; the honored dead lay in state in sturdy log vaults while offerings of goods and food were placed beside them; their bodies were painted with pigments such as ochre or red graphite; sometimes a canopy was erected over the open tomb. When the flesh had begun to decay, the heaping of earth began. Often a second burial took place on the site of an earlier one, so that some Adena mounds eventually grew to tremendous size.

Within these late mounds have been found such objects as "trophy" skulls—clean, sometimes polished skulls placed on the thighs of buried bodies. Another unusual Adena object is the antler headdress, previously thought to be a Hopewell trait. These were usually made of the skullcap and antlers of an actual deer or elk, but some were fashioned from thin hammered sheets. Were they ceremonial crowns? The insignia of a chief or priest?

Other impressive grave goods include the effigy pipes—such as the splendid human effigy from the Adena Mound; copper bracelets and rings; abstract forms cut from thick sheets of mica; masks that include animal bones and teeth; and the striking flat stone tablets, usually covered with

23   The Berlin tablet. Courtesy Ohio Historical Society,
Columbus, Ohio.

graceful, curving geometrical designs. About a dozen engraved tablets and twice that number of blank ones have
been recovered since the first was found in the Grave Creek
Mound in 1838. Webb and Snow think that the tablets may
have served as grinding stones for awls or knives used in
ceremonial bloodletting rituals. Others have suggested that
the tablets were used merely for stamping textiles.

The most conspicuous Adena object is one of the most
famous of all American mounds: the Great Serpent Mound
in Adams County, Ohio. No human artifacts have ever been
found in it, so its Adena origin is only a guess; but excavation of a burial mound some 400 feet from it has yielded
characteristic Adena objects, including a copper breastplate,
stone axes and points, and grooved pieces of sandstone.

The Serpent is the largest known serpent effigy in the
world. It consists of a low, rounded embankment nearly a
quarter of a mile long, in the form of a gigantic snake. The
serpent's head reaches a sheer rock precipice a hundred feet

above a creek; in seven great coils it writhes southward to its triple-coiled tail. Clasped in the serpent's open jaws is an oval, thought by some to represent an egg, by others a frog. The serpent is 1,254 feet long from tail to the tip of its upper jaw; the average width of the body is about 20 feet, its height four or five feet.

Today this monster is covered by a neat coat of grass and occupies the place of honor in a state park with adjoining picnic grounds. On a summer day hundreds of children swarm around the mound or climb the observation tower from which its whole length can be seen. Yet this remarkable work—strangest of all the mounds—nearly was destroyed in the last century. Only the efforts of a few dedicated individuals saved it.

The existence of the Great Serpent Mound has long been known. Atwater did not mention it, but Squier and Davis included a map of it in their survey. "No plan or description has hitherto been published," Squier wrote, "nor does the fact of its existence appear to have been known beyond the secluded vicinity in which it occurs." Squier discussed the use of serpent-and-globe symbols in Egypt, Greece, and other ancient civilizations, but did not try to trace Ohio's Serpent to possible Old World origins.

In the summer of 1883, F. W. Putnam of the Peabody Museum came to the Great Serpent. Describing his visit, he wrote of the awe he felt at seeing "the mysterious work of an unknown people whose seemingly most sacred place we had invaded. . . . There seemed to come to me a picture as of a distant time, and with it came a demand for an interpretation of this mystery. The unknown must become known."

The mound then belonged to a farmer who was aware

of its scientific importance and who had refrained from
planting crops on the site. But Putnam was worried about
the Great Serpent's future; already there was talk of leveling
the giant Cahokia Mound to get ballast for a railroad track,
and who knew what might happen to the Serpent if the
farmer sold his land?

In 1886, Putnam visited the Serpent again—a trip that in
those days took 7½ hours by railroad and carriage from
Cincinnati. He found the mound partly obliterated by
amateur excavators, the trampling of cattle and visitors, and
the effects of rain. And the farmer said he was about to sell;

24   The Great Serpent Mound. Aerial photograph, courtesy
     Museum of the American Indian, Heye Foundation,
     New York.

"THE SERPENT,"
[Entry 1014]
ADAMS COUNTY OHIO.
E. G. Squier & E. H. Davis Surveyor 1846.

25   The Serpent. Diagram, Squier and Davis, 1848.

the mound would almost certainly be turned into a corn-field then. Putnam managed to get a one-year option to buy the mound, and set out to raise the money for its purchase.

He began his campaign by writing to a Boston newspaper, "To me it seems a greater loss than would be the destruction of our own monument on Bunker Hill, and yet what indig-

nation would be aroused should some dynamite fiend topple
that to the ground!" A group of Bostonians raised $5,880,
and in June 1887, Putnam bought the mound for the Peabody Museum. That summer he spent eight weeks restoring
it to the condition it had been in when Squier and Davis had
made their chart 40 years before. He also built a fence with
a turnstile, and installed a hitching post and horse trough
for the convenience of visitors. In 1900, the Peabody Museum gave the Serpent to the Ohio Archaeological and
Historical Society to be maintained as a state park.

                                5

     For archaeologists there are three great unanswered
questions about the Adena Culture:
     How did it originate?
     What was its relationship to the Hopewell Culture?
     Why did it decline?
     It seems clear that the Adena people were intruders in
the Ohio Valley, representing not merely a new cultural
tradition but a new physical stock. The Archaic inhabitants
of the region were mainly long-headed, with narrow skulls
and slender bodies. They lived in riverbank villages, feeding
on shellfish, wild game, and seeds, and built no burial
mounds. The Adena folk were quite different.
     The first description of an Adena skull was provided by
Samuel Morton in his *Crania Americana* in 1839, though
of course the Adena Culture had not yet then been identified. He spoke of its "ponderous bony structure . . . large
jaws and broad face," and mentioned the flattened skull
produced by the pressure of a board bound against the head
in infancy.

Webb and Snow, 120 years later, described the Adena type as having a large round skull, prominent forehead, heavy brow ridges, jutting chin, and massive bones. The Adena folk were unusually tall; bones of women over six feet in height and men approaching seven feet have been discovered. This band of people of great majesty and size forced its way into the Ohio Valley about 1000 B.C., it seems. However, Webb and Snow add the cautious note that their picture of the Adena physical type is based on less than a hundred skulls, nearly all from the elaborately prepared late Adena log tombs. "The Adena people selected for the elaborate mound burial—the honored dead—cannot be regarded as representative samples of the Adena population," they point out. "It seems certain that many, if not most, of the ordinary people must have been cremated in the common form of burial preparation. Therefore we are dealing with a most unusual group."

Perhaps there was a small elite of round-headed giants dominating and ruling an existing long-headed Ohio Valley population. But the question remains: where did the mound-building Adenas come from?

Webb and Snow, in 1945, suggested Mexico. They based their theory on the presence of round-headed people in prehistoric Mexico, on the custom they also had of head-binding to flatten skulls, and on the mound-building traits of the Adena folk, which seemed derived from Mexican practices. This view has many supporters. Archaeologists who believe that the Adena people migrated from Mexico have supplied long lists of parallels between Adena culture and that of early Mexico—such as the use of trophy skulls in burials, tombs in earthen mounds, and the design of the carved tablets.

Attempts have been made to trace the supposed migration route from Mexico into the Ohio Valley. One suggestion is that the puzzling Poverty Point site in northern Louisiana may have been a place where the Adena people settled for a while on their way north. At Poverty Point, near the town of Floyd in West Carroll Parish, there is a cluster of six mounds. The largest is a flat-topped T-shaped structure 70 feet in height; the other mounds are from 4 to 21 feet high, and the entire group is laid out in a semicircle.

The Poverty Point mounds were first observed by an archaeologist in 1872, but little attention was paid to them until recent times, when the U. S. Army Engineers took aerial photos of the group while mapping the Mississippi River. In 1953, these photos were studied by James A. Ford, then on the staff of New York's American Museum of Natural History. Ford noticed an unusual geometrical arrangement no one had detected before.

It seemed to him that the worn ridges of today's Poverty Point mounds once were a set of six eight-sided figures, one within the next. At some distant time in the past a shift in the channel of the Arkansas River must have washed away the octagons' eastern side. A report that Ford and C. H. Webb published in 1956 estimated that the original structure may have been 11.2 miles long, 6 feet high, and 80 feet thick. This would require 530,000 cubic yards of earth, they calculated—35 times the volume of the Great Pyramid of Khufu in Egypt. The largest mound of this structure, Ford wrote, "is easily the most spectacular of the accomplishments of these people. It measures 700 by 800 feet at the base and rises to 70 feet above the surrounding plain . . . it can be estimated that the finished mound required something over three million man-hours of labor."

Ford's excavations suggested that the entire huge structure was built in a single effort, not over a long period of time. He estimates a population of several thousand, and calculates that it must have taken twenty million 50-pound basketloads of soil to construct the earthworks. Thus "this community must have been rather strictly organized. While a religious motivation may ultimately explain the large amount of earth construction, this effort was obviously well controlled. The geometrical arrangement of the town . . . [is clearly the result] of central planning and direction. . . ."

Carbon-14 dates for Poverty Point fell between 1200 and 100 B.C. Ford and Webb, who thought the site was a southern colony of the Adena or Hopewell culture, preferred an 800–600 B.C. date for the flourishing of the community, which would place it several centuries after the emergence of Adena. But the artifacts found at Poverty Point are pre-Adena, Archaic in type; the site would be considered Late Archaic except for the presence of those astonishing earthworks. No Adena or Hopewell material has been found. And, though it seems impossible that such vast works could have been constructed without the support of a farming economy, no traces of agriculture have been detected at Poverty Point; its inhabitants did not even have pots to cook in, but heated the water to prepare their food by dropping hot balls of baked clay into baskets containing water.

Several possibilities exist: that Poverty Point was a native Louisiana non-farming community which somehow took to building immense earthworks; that there was influence from Ohio; or that the site represents a settlement of northward-bound migrants who eventually reached the Ohio Valley and established the Adena Culture. Or perhaps Poverty

Point was a sacred ceremonial city. But for whom?

A good many archaeologists find the Mexico theory—including the stopping-off point in Louisiana—unacceptable. Don Dragoo, whose excavation of the Cresap Mound gave him unusual perspective on the whole range of Adena development, has pointed out that most of the "Mexican" traits found in Adena mounds come from *late* Adena mounds and are absent from those he has identified as early ones. If the Adena people came from Mexico, he says, it is strange that they failed to employ these "Mexican" traits for several hundred years after their arrival in Ohio, then began to use them. Dragoo questions the resemblances seen by others between Adena practices and the burial and skull-flattening customs of early Mexico. He points out the great differences between Mexican and Adena pottery styles. He finds the Mexican theory "romantic and thought-provoking," but declares that "the time has come for serious consideration of other possible sources for the roots of Adena."

Dragoo finds signs of those sources in certain Late Archaic sites in the Northeast and in the lower Great Lakes area. He bases much of his reasoning on the work of the New York archaeologist William A. Ritchie, who had found evidences of a burial cult at two New York sites. Mound building was unknown among these people, but the way they buried their dead seemed to foreshadow Adena customs.

From New York, Dragoo traces these early ideas into Archaic cultures in Illinois, Ohio, Indiana, and Michigan. He sees the Adena ideas perhaps developing in several places at once and gradually spreading over a wide region, each local culture contributing to the general pool of thought until a full-fledged new culture emerged. As for the unusual Adena physical type, he thinks it may not be typical of

Adena as a whole; when more skulls have been recovered from early Adena mounds, we may form a different idea of what these people looked like.

6

The question of Adena's relation to Hopewell also remains unsettled. Webb and Snow, in 1945, voiced the beliefs held by most archaeologists: that Adena was earlier than Hopewell; that Hopewell represented a stock of long-headed intruders who came into the territory controlled by the round-headed Adena folk; that the burial and earthwork customs of Hopewell were borrowed from Adena; that there was close contact and even intermarriage between Adena and Hopewell; and that all Adena sites had been abandoned before the greatest years of the Hopewell Culture. But Don Dragoo, as might be expected, questions much of this theory. He rejects the belief that Hopewell ideas were drawn from Adena, and thinks that Hopewell and Adena may have developed side by side.

The origin of Hopewell, like that of Adena, is in doubt. The Hopewells had the agile bodies and narrow-headed skulls typical of the Archaic population of the eastern woodlands; some authorities think that they first took form as a culture near the eastern end of Lake Ontario, moving down gradually into the Adena-held Ohio Valley. But others have suggested an origin in Illinois for Hopewell.

What was the impact on Hopewell as it infiltrated Adena territory? And what impact did the newcomers have on the Adena folk?

The traditional archaeological view is that Adena had already begun to develop the traits which became so special-

ized and highly artistic in Hopewell. These included such
things as the use of copper and mica, the carving of stone
and bone, log tombs, earthworks, and so forth. But Dragoo
points out that many of the traits which Hopewell supposedly borrowed from late Adena are missing in early
Adena. Who learned from whom? He thinks that the sudden
enrichment of life in late Adena times is largely the result
of Hopewell influence. Dragoo calls Hopewell "the catalyst"
that sparked the transformation and expansion that occurred
late in the Adena way of life.

By late Adena times, the Adena Culture was spread all
along the tributaries of the Ohio River, from southeastern
Indiana to western Pennsylvania. Hopewell's range at that
time was much more compact, centered chiefly in the Scioto
Valley of Ohio. Dragoo sees this Hopewell concentration as
a "wedge" driven into Adena territory from the northwest.
According to Webb and Snow, this "mixing and blending
of two different peoples brought about a hybrid vigor,
genetically and culturally," that resulted in the magnificence
of Ohio Hopewell.

After this collision, peaceful or otherwise, between the
two cultures, Hopewell grew and Adena steadily dwindled.
The Adena people of the Scioto Valley apparently were
swallowed up by the Hopewells. There was no opposition to
the spread of Hopewell westward through Indiana and
Illinois. But in Kentucky and West Virginia, it seems,
Adena resisted Hopewell and kept the newcomers out.

Perhaps as a result of Hopewell hostility, the late Adena
folk crowded together in large centers. Their culture, which
(if Dragoo is right) had been so greatly enriched by the
impact of Hopewell, grew conservative and sterile. Finally,
several centuries before Christ, those Adenas who had not

been drawn into the Hopewell Culture began a gradual exodus from the Ohio Valley.

Some Adena groups went south along the Tennessee River. Salvage archaeology work in northern Alabama in 1934, just before the construction of the TVA's Wheeler Dam, revealed a distinct burial-mound culture notable for its use of copper and of galena, the lustrous, brilliant ore of lead. William S. Webb, who was in charge of this work, gave these people the name Copena Culture (*cop*per-gal*ena*). They seem to have evolved out of the late Adena culture and perhaps were refugees from Ohio.

Other Adena bands went eastward to Maryland and even to upper New York State. Far from home, far from the ancestral mounds and sacred circles, these Adena outcasts found it increasingly difficult to practice their traditional way of life. They had brought prized possessions with them from Ohio: breastplates, beads, amulets. But the religion of the burial cult demanded that these be interred with the dead; as the older people died, the supply of these treasures diminished. The traditions crumbled. A ruined people could no longer find the energy and discipline needed to construct mounds and earthworks. Probably by the first century A.D. the Adena way of life was extinct in its Ohio Valley birthplace, and the outlying groups could not have survived much beyond that time. Those in New York and along the Atlantic coast gave up first; unable to maintain their old ways, forgetful of their great traditions, they let themselves be absorbed into local tribes. The Copena people hung on a few centuries longer; but by A.D. 400, probably, they had ceased to exist as a distinct cultural group.

By then the bell was tolling for Hopewell, too. The mound-building era in the Ohio Valley had come to an end.

7

The Hopewells were the Mound Builders of whom the nineteenth-century mythmakers dreamed. Though neither Phoenician nor Hindu nor Toltec, but merely long-headed American Indians out of the eastern woodlands, they met many of the qualifications for that phantom race of superior beings to whom the Ohio mounds had so often been credited.

They were the first empire builders of the United States. It is doubtful that there ever was such a thing as a Hopewell empire, a Hopewell nation, in the political sense; but there is no question that Hopewell cultural influence was widespread and that wherever it reached it became overwhelmingly dominant. Some archaeologists have written of an actual Hopewell state, ruled from a central capital in southern Ohio and extending its grasp westward across Indiana and Illinois into southeastern Iowa, northward to Wisconsin and Michigan, and southward down the Mississippi past St. Louis. A younger school of archaeologists has introduced the idea of a Hopewell "interaction sphere," held together by a common religion rather than by any central government. They compare it to the Moslem "interaction sphere" which spread out of Arabia to such diverse cultures as those of Turkey, Syria, Persia, and North Africa.

Whether it was a religious movement or—as most archaeologists still believe—a tightly unified culture, Hopewell's geographical range was enormous. Artifacts found in the Ohio mounds testify to Hopewell's even more impressive ability to send trade missions beyond its Midwestern heartland. Copper from the Upper Great Lakes, mica from the

Appalachians, volcanic glass from the Rockies or from the Southwest, conch shells from the Gulf Coast, other seashells from the Atlantic, grizzly-bear teeth from the Rockies, fossil shark teeth, silver, meteoritic iron, and other exotic materials show what a wide net the Hopewells were able to cast. The aim of all this activity, according to Olaf H. Prufer of Cleveland, a leader in modern Hopewell research, "appears to have been exclusively the production of ceremonial objects primarily intended for deposition with the dead."

The core of the Hopewell territory—the Scioto-Muskingum-Miami river system, tributary to the Ohio—was the

26   Map of Hopewell sites.

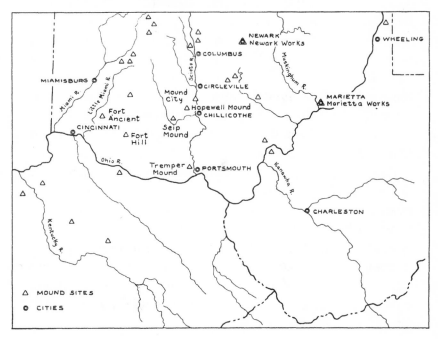

place of the great construction projects that so thoroughly
dazzled the minds and kindled the imaginations of our
forefathers: the thousands of burial mounds, the incredibly
huge embankments and ramparts and avenues. The greater
the distance of Hopewellian settlements from southern Ohio,
the weaker was the mound-building impulse; geometrical
enclosures are found almost exclusively in Ohio, and the
burial mounds become smaller and less well stocked with
artifacts on the margins of the Hopewellian territory. Possibly the outlying people never fully caught the spirit of the
religious movement that excited those in Ohio.

The name Hopewell Culture gives a sort of immortality
to Captain M. C. Hopewell of Ross County, Ohio, whose
farm near Chillicothe contained more than thirty mounds
within a 110-acre rectangular enclosure. When it was
decided to have an anthropological exhibit at the Chicago
World's Fair of 1893, Warren K. Moorehead excavated a
number of Ohio mounds; the richest haul of artifacts came
from Captain Hopewell's farm, and after the breakdown of
the old "Mound Builder" idea, the label "Hopewell" was
attached to all sites where similar artifacts were found.

Most of the mounds and earthworks that can be seen in
Ohio today were built by the Hopewells. The most awesome,
perhaps, is the great enclosure at Newark, which once
covered four square miles. The long parallel earthen-walled
avenues that so impressed Atwater and Squier have vanished, and only two important features of the Newark
works remain. One, the Great Circle Earthworks, serves as
a public fairground; it consists of an embankment about
1,200 feet in diameter, with earthen walls 8 to 14 feet high,
enclosing 26 acres. At the center of the circle is the so-called
Eagle Mound, a bird effigy.

A long earthen avenue, now gone, once connected the Great Circle with a large square enclosure a quarter of a mile away. Only a small section of this still exists. From it a second avenue led westward a considerable distance to the joined circle and octagon making up the finest part of the Newark works. The circle and octagon survive in Octagon State Memorial, the site of a municipal golf course. The low flat-topped mounds within the octagon serve now to test the skill of golfers, and the flags marking the eighteen holes mar the beauty and splendor of the scene only slightly. One walks across the flawless green grass of the golf course so stirred by the size and symmetry of the ancient site that one hardly feels like criticizing the use modern Newark has found for it.

Not many of the other geometrical enclosures that once existed can be seen today, but there is no shortage of Hopewell burial mounds. They are the most visible evidence of the complex cult of the dead that these people created. Here the sacred rites and ceremonies were performed; here the tribal notables were laid to rest in splendor. Some three fourths of the Hopewell dead were cremated; tomb burial in the flesh was seemingly the privilege only of a high caste.

A Hopewell funeral began with the clearing of trees and underbrush from the site where the mound was to rise; loose topsoil also was removed, and the subsurface usually was plastered with tough clay. Next, a layer of sand or fine gravel an inch or more in depth was strewn over the clay floor, and then a wooden-walled house for the dead was erected.

Burials of several kinds took place in the same house. Cremations were carried out in clay-lined pits in the floor; afterwards ashes and bone fragments were gathered up and placed in log crypts on platforms near the pits, or else were left in the pits.

In an adjoining chamber burials in the flesh were prepared. A tomb of logs was constructed on a low clay platform on the floor; the dead one lay stretched out within, surrounded by grave goods that had been "killed," or broken—presumably to liberate their spirits so that they could accompany the deceased into the afterworld. These log tombs were similar to the Adena tombs; the chief difference between Adena and Hopewell burials lies not in the preparation of the tombs but in the greater richness and quality of the Hopewell grave goods.

The individual graves within the funeral house were usually, though not always, covered with low mounds of earth. When the whole enclosure was filled with graves, it was deliberately set afire; then a great mound of earth was heaped over the entire site, sometimes while the embers of the burned funeral house still glowed. Probably the whole community took part in building the large mound. "Earth was carried in any convenient manner," wrote the Ohio archaeologist Henry C. Shetrone. "In detached clods, in carrying baskets, and doubtless even in buckskin aprons, each individual load being dumped upon the growing heap to add its little to the whole. The size, and often the form, of these individual loads are frequently readily discernible as exploration proceeds, owing to the fact that individual workers obtained their earth from various places, so that there appears a dumping of black soil here, a load of yellow clay there. . . . In two instances the writer has found individual loads intact, where the weary or careless worker had dropped them on the common heap 'basket and all.' "

One of the most important mound groups of the early Hopewell period is Mound City, near Chillicothe. Here twenty-four mounds lie within a 13-acre rectangular enclosure, whose earthen walls may once have been topped by a wooden fence. Some of the mounds are hardly more than little swellings on the earth, but the central mound is nearly 18 feet high.

Squier and Davis visited the site in 1846, digging shafts down through the summits of the mounds and extracting more than 200 handsome effigy pipes. Amateur pot-hunters

27   Mound City group. *Photograph by Barbara Silverberg.*

raided the mounds repeatedly thereafter, leaving many of them in poor repair. But real catastrophe came during World War I, when Mound City became Camp Sherman, a large military training center. Most of the mounds were leveled to make room for barracks, though a last-minute plea by the Ohio State Museum spared some. After the war, Camp Sherman was pulled down, and William C. Mills and Henry C. Shetrone of the Ohio Archaeological and Historical Society conducted extensive excavations at Mound City in 1920–21. Despite the destruction done by the army, the floors of many mounds containing the burial caches were still intact.

In one large mound Mills and Shetrone found twenty burials; four cremated bodies had been placed in a grave decked with thick sheets of mica. Today the so-called Mica Grave Mound has been cunningly fitted with a window so visitors can peer in and see the grave exactly as the archaeologists found it. Beyond it lies the Mound of the Pipes, where Squier and Davis found the treasures that are now in the British Museum. Farther on, one comes to the Death Mask Mound, in which Mills found burned fragments of a human skull. Dr. Raymond Baby of the Ohio State Museum pieced the fragments together thirty years later and showed that they formed a mask designed to slip over a face. The same mound yielded a collection of copper figures showing the human form, human hands, birds, turtles, and various animals.

At the opposite side of the site, in a mound partly demolished by the building of Camp Sherman, Mills and Shetrone uncovered six cremation burials; among the burial offerings were fragments of the tusks of mastodons or mammoths. It is easy to imagine the excitement this find

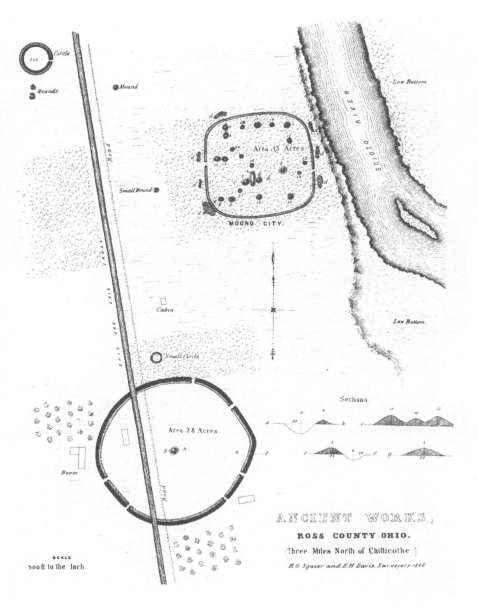

28　Diagram of the Mound City works. Squier and Davis,
1848.

would have caused if it had been made in the nineteenth century; but by 1920 it was clear that there had never been a face-to-face encounter between Hopewell man and the mastodon. These tusk fragments were already fossilized when they were discovered by the Indians, who revered them for reasons beyond our knowing.

After Mills and Shetrone finished their Mound City work in 1921, they restored the mounds to their nineteenth-century condition. The charts of Squier and Davis were valuable in this project. The 55-acre tract on which Mound City is situated became a state park after World War I, and in 1923 it came under national ownership as Mound City Group National Monument. Today the site is tranquil and seemingly unspoiled—deceptively so, for the present mounds are only replicas of the originals, hiding all the scars of the recent past.

The same is true of the great Seip Mound in Ross County, Ohio. This is the second largest Hopewell mound, exceeded only by the central mound of the Hopewell Group itself. It is 30 feet high, 250 feet long, and 150 feet wide. Today it stands in solitary majesty at the end of a long, narrow grassy field beside the highway, and it is hemmed in on both sides by private property; originally it was flanked by several minor mounds, and stood within a square enclosure and two circular earthworks. Only remnants of these are left. Shetrone spent three summers at Seip, from 1926 through 1928, and took the mound completely apart. The most striking discovery was a log vault containing the skeletons of four adults and two infants. Perhaps this was the tomb of tribal "royalty"; certainly its occupants had been important people, for they were buried along with thousands of pearls, and tools and ornaments of copper, mica, tortoise-shell, and

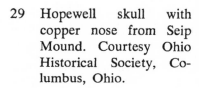

29 Hopewell skull with copper nose from Seip Mound. Courtesy Ohio Historical Society, Columbus, Ohio.

silver. Newspapers nicknamed the tomb "the great pearl burial."

One unusual burial feature was a skull adorned with an artificial copper nose; copper rods about a foot long lay near the skull, and evidently had once been attached to the hair. A few years earlier Shetrone had found a double burial at the Hopewell Group that displayed the same bizarre artificial copper noses. Other Seip Mound finds included a ceremonial copper ax weighing 28 pounds, a set of copper breastplates, and a well-preserved burial shroud in whose woven fabric could still be seen abstract designs in tan, maroon, and black. At the conclusion of the work, the Seip Mound was restored to its original dimensions. Nonetheless, the mound as seen today was assembled by archaeologists, not by prehistoric Indians, and this is a touchy point. Excavation means destruction. In order to find out what is in a mound, archaeologists must open it and, if they are to do their work properly, they must level it to its base. Even if they use the same soil afterward to

build a mound of the original size and shape, is it truly
the same mound?

The Hopewell Group was excavated in 1891–92 by
Warren K. Moorehead on behalf of the Chicago World's
Fair, and again between 1922 and 1925 by Henry Shetrone
for the Ohio State Museum. Here Shetrone, after excavating
more than 30 mounds, for various reasons was unable to
restore them immediately. Unfortunately a complete restoration was never undertaken.

Squier and Davis excavated four mounds of the group,
which they called the North Fork group because it was located on the north fork of Paint Creek. At the time, the
land belonged to a certain W. C. Clark; when Atwater had
visited the group a quarter of a century earlier, it had been

30 Pottery head from Seip
Mound, Hopewell culture.
Courtesy Ohio Historical
Society, Columbus, Ohio.

owned by a Mr. Ashley and a Colonel Evans. So it is only an accident of time that the Hopewell Culture is not known to us as the Clark or the Ashley-Evans Culture. Atwater thought that "the immense labour, and the numerous cemeteries filled with human bones, denote a vast population near this spot in ancient times," and Squier wrote, "The amount of labor expended in the construction of this work . . . is immense. The embankments measure together nearly *three miles* in length; and a careful computation shows that, including mounds, not less than three million cubic feet of earth were used in their composition."

From Mound No. 1 of the Hopewell Group, then reduced by plowing to a height of only three feet, Squier and Davis took a remarkable collection of artifacts: "Several coiled serpents, carved in stone, and carefully enveloped in sheet mica and copper; pottery; carved fragments of ivory [actually bone]; a large number of fossil teeth; numerous fine sculptures in stone, etc." Another mound produced thin, finely made blades of the volcanic glass called obsidian, scrolls cut from mica, woven cloth, bone needles, pearls, and many other things.

Moorehead's examination of the same mounds showed that Squier and Davis had scarcely exhausted the Hopewell Group. Squier and Davis had found a cache of some 600 flint disks, apparently having some religious purpose; Moorehead found 7,000 more. In another mound he came on over 50 burials, near which were found human jawbones that had been cut and perforated as ornaments and trophies. But in the great central mound—*the* Hopewell Mound—Moorehead made his most important finds. He drove five trenches across this mound, which was 500 feet long, 180 feet wide and 33 feet high, thus disclosing some 150 burials, accom-

31   Gooseneck effigy pipe from Hopewell Mound Group.
     Courtesy Ohio Historical Society, Columbus, Ohio.

32   Frog effigy pipe, Hopewell culture. Courtesy Museum
     of the American Indian, Heye Foundation, New York.

33   Owl effigy pipe, Hopewell cul-
     ture. Courtesy Museum of the
     American Indian, Heye Foun-
     dation, New York.

34 Alligator effigy pipe from
Esch Mound. Hopewell cul-
ture. Courtesy Ohio Historical Society, Columbus, Ohio.

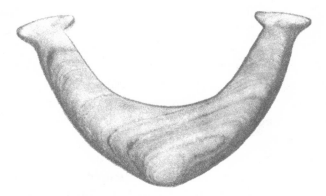

35 Bannerstone, Hopewell culture. Courtesy Museum of
the American Indian, Heye Foundation, New York.

36 Copper fish, Hopewell culture. Courtesy Field Museum
of Natural History, Chicago.

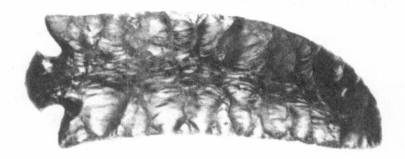

37 Obsidian ceremonial blade from Hopewell Mound Group. Courtesy Museum of the American Indian, Heye Foundation, New York.

panied by a rich assortment of copper offerings: circular, square, and diamond-shaped figures, effigies of fish and birds, serpent heads, and more, along with 67 copper axes (one weighing 38 pounds), and 23 copper breastplates. An offering beside an "altar" included "mica ornaments, spool-shaped ear ornaments, copper balls, many other copper objects, large beads, bears' and panthers' teeth, carved bones, effigies carved out of stone, stone tablets, slate ornaments, beautiful stone and terra-cotta rings, quartz crystals worked into various forms, flint knives, and cloth." A striking headdress with imitation deer antlers made of copper-covered wood came to light, along with artistically engraved human bones and ornaments made from the shells of ocean-going turtles.

Thirty years later, Shetrone arrived to begin his four summers of work at the Hopewell Group. He explored all existing mounds and demonstrated that this amazing city of the dead was not yet fully drained of treasure.

"In Mound 11," Shetrone wrote, "the Museum survey found a unique deposit. Alongside a crematory basin reposed the charred remains of a skeleton, accompanied by ornaments of mica and pearls. Adjacent to the burial was a large deposit of several hundred pounds of obsidian or volcanic glass. Encircling the burial . . . was a border of boulders. The obsidian was in fragments, chunks, and chips, clearly the raw material used in fashioning obsidian knives and ceremonial spear- and arrowpoints. . . . The nearest source of obsidian supply was known to be the Rocky Mountains." Archaeologists had wondered whether the Hopewell craftsmen had manufactured the obsidian goods themselves, or if they had been obtained ready-made from tribes in the West. Here was the answer: "Many of the fragments of the raw material displayed bruised and battered edges, the result of its being carried pickaback halfway across the continent from the far-distant source of supply. It seems logical to suppose that the burial in this mound was that of the master flint-chipper of the community and that the material of his craft had been buried with him as a tribute to his important office."

The double burial in the central Hopewell Mound,

38 Bird claw in Mica, Hopewell culture. Courtesy Field Museum of Natural History, Chicago.

marked by the presence of the artificial copper noses, was, said Shetrone, "an imposing example of barbaric splendor." A tall young man and a young woman lay side by side. "At the head, neck, hips, and knees of the female and completely encircling the skeleton were thousands of pearl beads and buttons of wood and stone covered with copper; extending the full length of the grave along one side was a row of copper ear ornaments; at the wrists of the female were copper bracelets; copper ear ornaments adorned the ears of both, and both wore necklaces of grizzly-bear canines and copper breastplates on the chest."

Room after room in the Ohio State Museum in Columbus is filled with exhibit cases packed with Hopewell grave goods, and this is only a fraction of what has been found. The immense quantity and high quality of these objects reveal much about Hopewell life: the wealth of the Ohio mound builders; the skill of their artisans; the taste for exotic raw materials that brought far-flung trade routes into being; and above all the incredible fascination with death, the powerful desire to send the dead into the next world accompanied by treasure. The Hopewells are the Egyptians of the United States, packing their earthen "pyramids" with a dazzling array. A single deposit from the Turner mounds in Hamilton County, Ohio, contained 12,000 unperforated pearls, 35,000 pearl beads, 20,000 shell beads, and nuggets of copper, meteoritic iron, and silver, as well as small sheets of hammered gold, copper and iron beads, and other things as well.

There is a stunning vigor about Ohio Hopewell. By comparison, the grave deposits of the Adena folk look sparse and poor. Hopewell displays a love of excess that shows itself not only in the intricate geometrical enclosures and

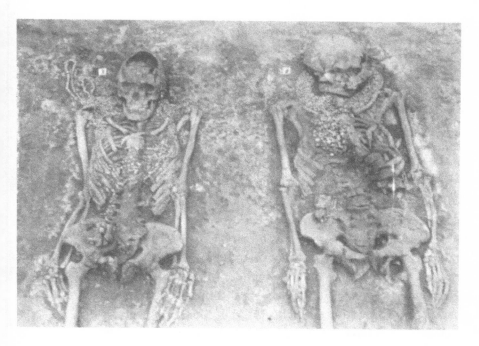

39   A Hopewell burial showing necklaces. Courtesy Illinois
State Museum, Springfield, Illinois.

in the massive mounds, but in the gaudy displays in the
tombs. To wrap a corpse from head to foot in pearls, to
weigh it down in many pounds of copper, to surround it
with masterpieces of sculpture and pottery, and then to
bury everything under tons of earth—this is the kind of
wastefulness that only an amazingly energetic culture would
indulge in.

8

What kept this enormously vital, exuberant culture going? Surely these people must have had a well-developed
agriculture, since a group so concerned with making fine

objects, conducting complex burial ceremonies, and erecting colossal mounds can hardly have had much time for hunting, fishing, and gathering wild nuts and fruits. Yet archaeologists have long been disturbed by the lack of any evidence that the Hopewells were farmers—or even that they had permanent settled villages.

Cyrus Thomas called attention to this in 1894, concluding that "the houses of the mound-builders were constructed of perishable materials." True; but even perishable huts leave traces that archaeologists can usually detect. Intensive field work over more than a century has revealed only about half a dozen Ohio Hopewell settlements, none of them near any of the great ceremonial centers. And only at two Ohio Hopewell sites were traces of corn found. This led to the seemingly impossible conclusion that the Hopewells were nomads who lived by simple hunting and fishing, coming together at certain significant moments to create the great earthen structures and then wandering off again.

Clearly it was absurd to think of the magnificent Hopewells as living in an Archaic-style food-gathering culture; but perhaps the Hopewells simply did not need to live near their mounds. Dragoo's work at the Cresap Mound had demonstrated that Adena folk constructed their mounds over many generations, adding new burials to them and increasing their bulk; in other words the Adenas lived near their mounds and had a close relationship with them over periods that may have lasted for centuries. But, as Olaf Prufer of the Case Institute of Technology showed, this was not the situation with the Hopewells.

With two exceptions, their mounds had each been built in a single stage. This was apparent not only from the structure of each mound, but also from carbon-14 dating.

"The dates are so closely spaced for different features in the mound," Prufer wrote, "that it is far easier to conclude from them that they apply to a structure built at one go." And so the many burials in the Hopewell mounds must have been entombed within a short time of one another. "It is difficult to believe," said Prufer, "that these dead people all belong to the same family or clan having died at the same time. Such a thing could be possible in one or two cases, but we are dealing here with a repetitive pattern that can be traced from site to site, from mound to mound." He suggested that whenever a great man died, his servants or slaves were forced to accompany him into the grave.

But where were the Hopewell villages? Prufer, who was convinced that the Hopewells had been farmers, began in 1962 to look for Hopewell village sites away from the mounds—in the rich bottomlands along the rivers. Perhaps, he thought, the mounds were religious centers that were deserted most of the time, with the Hopewells leaving their small farming communities to go to them only at certain great ritual occasions.

He led survey teams through the valleys of the Ohio basin and turned up 37 small village sites, the largest one not much more than 100 feet wide. Typical Hopewell utensils were strewn near the surface. A farmer named Alva McGraw told Prufer of another such site on his property along the Scioto River, two miles south of Chillicothe, that was soon to be destroyed by road construction. Prufer dug an exploratory trench there and found that he had come upon the answer to one of the major Hopewell mysteries. Eight inches down lay a foot-thick deposit of ancient village debris 95 by 140 feet in area. It contained more than 10,000 pottery fragments, 2,000 mollusk shells, remains of wild plants, and both a whole ear and individual kernels of corn. Numerous Hopewell artifacts were uncovered.

The McGraw site told Prufer that the Hopewells had indeed been farmers, raising corn, the most valuable of early American crops. It revealed the other elements of their diet: deer, rabbit, and turkey meat; hickory nuts and acorns, wild plums, turtles, fish, shellfish. Carbon-14 dating and other evidence suggested A.D. 450 as the date of the operation of the McGraw site—late in Hopewell times.

The site yielded ornaments of the kind found in Hopewell graves, along with some artifacts of a non-Hopewell type. Prufer believes that the McGraw-site people who made the Hopewell-type ornaments were not the same as those who were buried in the great Hopewell mounds. He thinks the McGraw craftsmen may have been Ohio Adena people and suggests that the Hopewell religion was brought to Ohio from Illinois by "a privileged minority who in some way had come to dominate some of Ohio's Adena people, among whom were the farmers of the McGraw site." Imposing their religion on the established tribes of Ohio and surrounding states, these long-headed Hopewell intruders introduced new artistic styles as well as new burial customs, and turned the river-bottom settlements into workshops to produce the wealth that went into the mounds of their great chieftains. This theory has the advantage of explaining why Hopewell villages were so remote from Hopewell ceremonial centers.

The origin of Hopewell life is a controversial matter. Ohio Hopewell carbon-14 dates show the culture taking form about 500 B.C., reaching its peak between 100 B.C. and A.D. 200, and disappearing between A.D. 550 and 750. This is roughly the same length of time that Adena lasted, Hopewell beginning and ending some five centuries later than Adena with a considerable overlap between late Adena and classic Hopewell. As with Adena, many archaeologists see a Mexican origin for the Hopewell traits, and many others regard them as an outgrowth of purely local developments in the eastern United States during the Archaic Period. (And some archaeologists believe that the Hopewells borrowed their entire culture from the Adenas, markedly developing Adena traits, as the Romans developed Greek traits.)

The work of Olaf Prufer and his colleagues produces a picture of the long-headed Hopewells moving out of the Northeast into Illinois and then into Ohio, picking up useful traits as they went and creating in Ohio a dynamic cultural center whose influence radiated outward over a wide area. The starting point of this movement may have been in Ontario and central New York State, about 800 or 1000 B.C. Artifacts and burial mounds in what seems to be a very early Hopewell style have been found in New York.

But there may also have been influence on Hopewell development coming from Mexico. The early Hopewells may have learned from Mexico the techniques of raising corn, and perhaps also picked up in the same way the idea of gigantic earthworks. It is possible to list many traits common to both Hopewell and early Mexican culture—earplugs, burial mounds, head-flattening, log tombs, the use of mica, and so on. Though most archaeologists are cautious about drawing conclusions from these similarities, one—Edward V. McMichael of West Virginia—is convinced "that the climax of Ohio Valley Hopewell was stimulated by Mexican influences and that the mechanism for this influence was the Crystal River Complex of the Floridian Gulf Coast." He outlined his theory in 1961.

The Crystal River Complex is a prehistoric culture whose sites are found along Florida's Gulf Coast from Tampa to the mouth of the Apalachicola River, and are also found inland for some 150 miles. The chief site, at Crystal River, is four miles from the Gulf. It includes two large temple mounds with ramps, a small residential mound, two burial mounds, and a plaza. Clarence B. Moore excavated the main burial mound and its surrounding platform in 1903 and 1906, discovering 411 burials and a rich collection of shell ornaments, copper objects, and other artifacts. Later this culture was shown to extend over a broad stretch of Florida. Many of its traits seem clearly akin to late Hopewell. Carbon-14 dates for Crystal River Complex sites range from 537 B.C. to about A.D. 1 (with a possible error of 150 years in either direction).

There is no doubt about contact between Hopewell and Crystal River. Flint knives of the Hopewell type have been found in Florida, and pottery from Florida has been found in Ohio; and many objects unearthed in Ohio are almost identical to objects unearthed in Florida. It was long thought that Crystal River was a Hopewell-influenced settlement, but McMichael would reverse this, saying that the flow of ideas ran from south to north. He points to the flat-topped mounds at Crystal River. Such mounds were unknown to the Adena folk and were not built by the early Hopewells; but they appear at such Hopewell sites as Marietta and Newark. McMichael thinks that the Hopewells experimented with flat-topped mounds after learning about them in Florida—and that the Crystal River people were in direct contact with the Mexican civilization centered around Veracruz.

Several sites near Veracruz have yielded cultural traits that seem linked to Crystal River and Hopewell. The site most frequently discussed as a possible point of origin for the Ohio Valley mound-building concepts is La Venta, situated on a small island in a swamp near the Tonalá River, about a dozen miles inland from the Gulf of Mexico. Known to archaeologists since 1925, La Venta was first extensively explored just before World War II, when several huge mounds and rectangular enclosures were examined. In 1955 the National Geographic Society and the University of California sponsored further work there under the direction of Philip Drucker and Robert F. Heizer. They found an elaborate series of structures centering around the main "pyramid," a clay mound 240 by 420 feet at the base, and over 100 feet high. Drucker has suggested that the island of La Venta was a sacred shrine inhabited by a group of priests and their servants, and visited regularly by worshipers from the surrounding region.

Many of La Venta's treasures were meant to be buried as soon as they were created. "Under tons of clay," wrote Drucker and Heizer, "went carefully worked figurines, their most precious gems, their gaudiest monuments. In one corner of La Venta's main Ceremonial Court, for instance, we uncovered a magnificent 15½-foot-square mask of the jaguar god. It was composed of 486 neatly cut squares of green serpentine, its mouth stained with brilliant orange sand. . . . Yet seemingly no sooner was the mask finished than it was covered, first with a coating of olive-colored clay and then with some 500 additional tons of pink clay.

Above ground at La Venta they left only pyramided mounds, sculptured monuments, platforms, and columns marking courts and submerged mosaics." The archaeologists believed that La Venta was occupied from about 800 B.C. to about A.D. 400. Then it was apparently destroyed. It remained a holy place for hundreds of years thereafter, but its temples and courts were deserted, visited only by pilgrims who hurriedly buried their offerings and fled.

McMichael thinks that traders or colonists voyaged in large canoes across the Gulf of Mexico from northern Veracruz to the northwest coast of Florida and that the ideas that then took root at Crystal River were passed along to the Hopewells before A.D. 1. Partial proof of this was provided by Ripley P. Bullen of the Florida State Museum in 1965; he discovered two stone columns almost certainly inspired by Mexican styles. Their carbon-14 dates are too late for them to have had any influence on the development of Ohio Hopewell, but if Mexicans were in Florida in A.D. 440 when these columns were carved, there is no reason that they could not have been there five or six hundred years earlier.

At present we can give no firm answer to the question of Hopewell origins. It now seems that the Hopewells emerged from the obscurity of the woodlands, borrowed some ideas from the Adenas, some from distant Mexico, thought up some themselves, and drew them all together to create a dazzling, wealthy society that flourished for centuries, indulged in splendid burial customs unknown elsewhere in the prehistoric United States, imposed its way of life on an area covering thousands of square miles, sent traders to the shores of far-off seas, amassed great treasure to thrust into earthen mounds, erected phenomenal structures in geometrical patterns—and faded away, leaving behind the ramparts and mounds that aroused such wonder in our great-grandfathers.

9

The end of Hopewell, like the end of any great culture, holds a special fascination. By A.D. 550—perhaps even earlier—the Hopewells had ceased to build their ceremonial centers. In another two centuries their distinctive way of life had disappeared, their territory was almost empty, and the remaining Hopewells had been absorbed into humbler tribes. We do not know what caused the abrupt crumbling of Hopewell. One authority, James B. Griffin, has suggested that changes in climate caused repeated crop failures and weakened the Hopewell economy. Others have guessed at famine, plague, civil war, and invasion of Hopewell territory by savage tribes. One theory is just about as good as another at this point in our knowledge.

In the nineteenth century, men looked at Ohio's hilltop ramparts and quickly saw why the Mound Builders had disappeared. Surely they had been attacked by barbarians and taken to the hills, and in the end had been defeated and wiped out. That is why such writers as Josiah Priest told how "the remnant of a tribe or nation . . . making a last struggle against the invasion of an overwhelming foe . . . perished amid the yells of their enemies."

These ramparts evidently *were* forts, and probably they mark the opening of the final phase of Hopewell life. Fort Ancient is the most impressive of these structures that we can see today. It occupies a long, narrow plateau several hundred feet above the Little Miami River in Warren

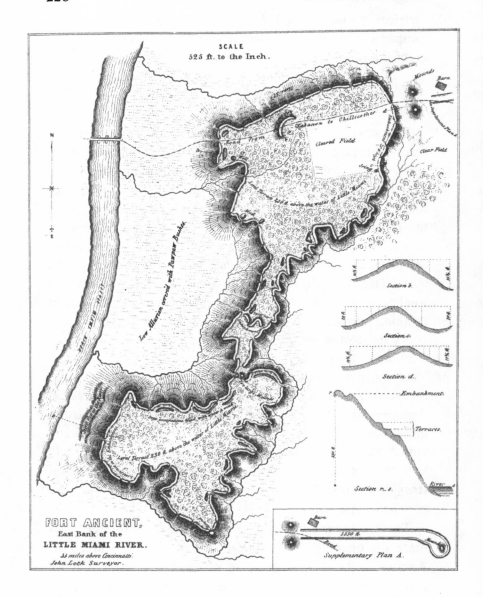

40   Diagram of Fort Ancient. Squier and Davis. 1848.

County, Ohio. The fort's earthen walls follow the edge of the plateau, which drops off steeply on the east and west and is bordered by deep ravines to the north and south. The only level approach is on the northeast, where the builders erected especially high walls to keep intruders out. Today State Route 350 pierces those walls.

The fort has three sections—the North Fort, the Middle Fort, and the South Fort—embracing about 100 acres in all. The walls forming these sections have a total length of more than three and a half miles, and the distance from the north end of Fort Ancient to the south end is nearly 5,000 feet. Middle Fort is merely an isthmus linking the larger enclosures on north and south; in the nineteenth century many persons theorized that the fort was a miniature model of North, Central, and South America. .

The outer walls, 20 feet high in some places and only 6 or 7 in others, are many feet thick. They are composed of earth and clay taken from a ditch that runs along their inner border, and here and there they are reinforced with flat stones, apparently to prevent erosion. The walls are broken by 70 openings, or "gateways," some caused by flood and storm, but most of them apparently intentional. Probably only 5 or 6 of these gaps actually were gateways, the others having once been blocked by wooden palisades.

Within the North Fort are six small burial mounds. A low crescent gateway separates it from the Middle Fort, which has a second crescent gateway at its southern end leading to the Great Gateway into the South Fort. To the west of this Great Gateway is a burial mound. Outside the fort proper are several other mounds and the largely destroyed remains of a walled avenue.

The State of Ohio has owned Fort Ancient since 1891;

today it is part of the 680-acre Fort Ancient State Memorial. Erosion damage has been repaired, and some mounds and sections of wall that excavators had torn down have been restored. Today Fort Ancient is an inviting place with smooth, rolling lawns and gently curving walls. Picnic tables stand where Hopewell chieftains once swaggered in pomp and glory.

Fort Hill in Highland County, Ohio, shows us a Hopewell fort as our ancestors would have seen it: unexcavated, unrestored, covered with forest so heavy that the fort's outlines are almost concealed. Fort Ancient, handsome as it is, has the air of being a museum exhibit; Fort Hill and some of the other surviving hilltop enclosures seem to have ghosts lingering in their tumbled underbrush.

Several small settlements have been discovered at the base of Fort Hill, suggesting that the Hopewells did not remain continuously shut up in their forts, but took refuge in them only at times of severe crisis. What such a crisis might be, we cannot guess; but Olaf Prufer notes that about the year A.D. 600 Indians in more northerly areas began to protect their villages with stockades, and "unrest of some kind appears to have been afoot throughout eastern North America."

This unrest may have triggered Hopewell's collapse by cutting off the supplies of imported raw materials that were so important to the religious cult. "Could the scheme itself be kept alive when the goods were no longer available?" Prufer asks. "I suggest that the Hopewell cult could survive only as long as its trade network remained intact and, further, that the postulated current of unrest in eastern North America during the seventh and eighth centuries A.D.

was sufficient to disrupt that network. Whether or not this caused the collapse of the Hopewell cult, there is no question that it did collapse. By the beginning of the Late Woodland period, about A.D. 750, elaborate burial mounds containing rich funeral offerings were no longer built." (Some archaeologists think the collapse of Hopewell came several centuries earlier than Prufer's date.)

The next developments in the Ohio Valley are unclear. Possibly there was actual emigration from the region; certainly there was a sharp decline in population. Some time after the end of Hopewell, the "Intrusive Mound Culture" appeared—so called because it buried its dead in graves dug into the tops and sides of old Hopewell mounds. These were simple hunting folk of the forest, probably unrelated to the Hopewells. Much later—about A.D. 1200, perhaps—the misnamed Fort Ancient Culture emerged. These people lived in and around Fort Ancient, but of course were not its builders. The Fort Ancient people dwelt in small villages of a few dozen bark-covered huts, raised corn, beans, squash, and sunflowers, and made modest pottery. Occasionally they interred one of their dead in a burial mound, but they were not really a mound-building culture, and possibly they felt a certain awe as they moved among the great structures, some already more than a thousand years old, that studded their area.

Perhaps the Fort Ancient people were actual descendants of the Ohio Hopewells. But so far there has been no way of tracing the line of descent from Hopewell through Fort Ancient to the historic Indian tribes. When white men arrived in Ohio late in the eighteenth century, they found only simple farming tribes, along with still simpler tribes that did not even practice agriculture. The white intruders dismissed the possibility that these folk could ever have built the great mounds and enclosures. So they invented mythical Mound Builders of non-Indian blood, and wove fabulous tales about them, while outraged Hopewell ghosts looked on in silent fury.

▲▲▲7

THE TEMPLE MOUND PEOPLE

▲▲▲

The mound-building impulse did not perish with the collapse of Ohio Hopewell. Hopewellian influence lingered in outlying regions; perhaps there was an actual migration of the Ohio people to such places as New York, Kansas, Michigan, and Wisconsin.

In some of these fringe areas of what is known as the Burial Mound II Period, mounds shaped in animal effigies and other odd forms were constructed. Not much connects these effigy-mound people to Hopewell. Most of the effigy mounds were built quite late, maybe even in the seventeenth or eighteenth century, a thousand years or more after the end of Ohio Hopewell. They represent a distorted echo of the basic mound concept. These impoverished cultures, heaping earth together in curiously-shaped low hillocks, have little in common with the splendor of classic Hopewell.

However, in the southeastern United States some centuries after the end of Hopewell, the mound idea reappeared in a quite different form. Once again great ceremonial centers were erected; once more an elaborate social system came into being; there were developments in art and in

technology that rivaled and often surpassed Hopewell at its
finest. But the cult of the dead was absent; the new mounds
were not burial mounds, and there was no urge to send
the dead into the next world accompanied by incredible
treasures. In no real way were the Temple Mound cultures
of the Southeast descended from Hopewell; though some
Hopewell ideas can be seen in these new cultures, it was
more a case of independent invention than of direct trans-
mission of ideas.

This new mound-building phase falls within a new cultural tradition that replaced the Woodland Tradition in
the eastern United States. Archaeologists call this new way
of life, which began to establish itself about A.D. 700, the
Mississippian Tradition.

The defining traits of the Woodland Tradition are the
use of pottery, a combined hunting and farming economy,
and the observance of a cult of the dead, including elaborate
rituals of burial and the establishment of ceremonial funeral
centers. The Mississippian Tradition, writes Gordon Willey
in his 1966 survey of contemporary archaeological ideas,
was quite different: "It was marked by rectangular, flat-
topped platform mounds which served as bases for temples,
chiefs' houses, and other important buildings. Frequently
these platform mounds were arranged around rectangular
open plazas. Although burial mounds did not disappear entirely in Mississippian cultures, they were dwarfed by the
platform mounds and were relatively minor features at the
major sites. Generally, in both earthwork construction and
extent of settlement, Mississippian sites were larger than
Woodland sites. Although large Adena and Hopewell
mound and embankment groups have been found and the
Poverty Point site in Louisiana is unusually large, it is

nevertheless true that the largest of the Mississippian centers, such as Cahokia (Illinois) or Moundville (Alabama), are even larger than these." Also, the dense accumulations of refuse at the Mississippian villages indicates that they were occupied for long periods by people who depended mainly on farming for their food supply.

The Mississippian Tradition, it will be recalled, is a term used to describe a particular group of cultural traits. It does not refer to any one culture or any one era in time. The years during which this tradition flourished in one place or another run from A.D. 700 to 1700; this span of a thousand years is termed the Temple Mound Period, subdivided into Temple Mound I and II.

The heartland of the Mississippian Tradition was the central Mississippi Valley—northeastern Arkansas, southeastern Missouri, southern Illinois, and western Tennessee. From here Mississippian ideas radiated up the rivers as far as the Great Lakes. A second Mississippian heartland in the lower Mississippi Valley developed about the same time, spreading through Alabama, Georgia, and the other Gulf Coast states. Beyond much doubt, the basic Mississippian ideas came from Mexico. The main Mississippian concept was that of the flat-topped, steep-sided temple mound, an earthen pyramid 80 to 100 feet high, covering many acres and bearing a wooden temple at its summit. This development in the United States followed shortly in time the start of a great pyramid-building movement in Mexico; we can still see splendid examples of it at such Mayan centers as Chichén Itzá in Yucatán. But there is no evidence of a mass migration of Mexicans into the United States; the contact was probably indirect, in the form of visits by Mexican traders to the Gulf Coast of the United States.

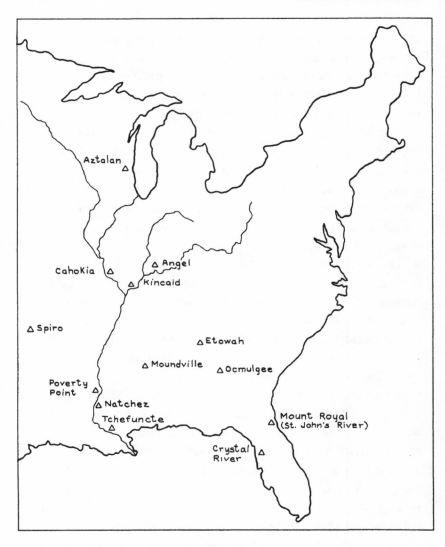

41   Map of Temple Mound sites.

The Southeast went through a long Archaic Tradition phase, which gave way to the Woodland Tradition about 1000 B.C. During the centuries when the big news in American life was being made in the Ohio Valley by Adena and then by Hopewell, the Southeast was occupied by much simpler folk, observing the Woodland way of life but building no mounds, except for some small isolated burial mounds of sand or earth.

At this time, also, certain outposts on the Gulf Coast were apparently exposed to direct contact with Mexico. The Crystal River Culture, already mentioned, is the most significant of these. Crystal River likewise had contact with Ohio. Whether ideas passed up the Mississippi from Crystal River to Hopewell or came down to Florida from Ohio is still unclear, but in any event various Hopewellian ideas began to circulate in the Southeast. Cultural life there became much richer, as is shown in the remarkably beautiful pottery produced then. Burial practices also grew more complex, undoubtedly a result of a spread of Hopewell ideas.

The Burial Mound I Period (1000–300 B.C.) saw the development of a number of Southeastern cultures showing signs of Hopewell influence. Among them was the Tchefuncte Culture of Louisiana, with its dome-shaped burial mounds as high as 15 feet and sometimes more than 100 feet in diameter. In early Burial Mound II (300 B.C.–A.D. 700) the Marksville Culture developed in Louisiana and spread over much of the lower Mississippi Valley. The Marksville people, who seem to have had much contact with Hopewell in its greatest era, buried their dead in large conical mounds, some of them 25 feet high and 150 feet in diameter at the base. One Marksville site shows the remnants of a semicircular earthen embankment 10 feet high which had served as an enclosure for the mounds and a plaza. This is a strikingly Hopewellian feature.

Sometime after A.D. 300, the Marksville Culture was succeeded in Louisiana by the Troyville Culture, which was quite similar in many ways. Troyville sites are generally larger than Marksville ones, though the burial mounds tend to be smaller. Troyville artifacts include ear spools made of copper from the Great Lakes region, perforated bear teeth, pipes, and other objects familiar from Hopewellian sites. The influence of Troyville has been detected in Texas, Arkansas, Mississippi, Alabama, and Florida. Toward the end of the Troyville Culture, pyramidal temple mounds appeared; thus many archaeologists regard Troyville as an example of the change from a burial-mound-building Woodland Tradition culture to a platform-mound-building Mississippian Tradition culture.

The next distinct Louisiana culture, Coles Creek, is definitely Mississippian. It is marked by fine, imaginative pottery designs; by large villages; and by ceremonial centers consisting of groups of flat-topped pyramids with temples at their summits. These mounds, 40 to 80 feet high, and as large as 200 feet square at the base, had ramps leading to their tops, and were arranged about a large central plaza.

The same cultural shift has been observed at many other sites over an enormous geographical range. In Illinois, a Woodland Tradition settlement was replaced by the Mississippian village that raised the immense Cahokia Mound. In eastern Tennessee there appeared an early Mississippian culture known as Hiwassee Island, typified by stockaded towns containing platform mounds and dwellings; ramps or stairs led up the sides of the mounds to the buildings on top, which had fireplaces, small platforms (altars?), and seats. The new tradition also spread through Georgia, Alabama, Florida, and surrounding states. The northernmost reach of the Mississippian Tradition was southern Wisconsin, where the great Aztalan Mounds of Jefferson County were built. Aztalan consists of an earthwork enclosing two pyramidal platform mounds; the whole site, which once was fortified by a palisade of clay-covered logs, covers some 10,000 square yards. Aztalan was probably a colonial offshoot of the Cahokia settlement.

The Mississippian Tradition's western expansion carried it into Texas, Arkansas, and Oklahoma, where the Caddo Culture took form. This culture is named for the Indians who were in possession of parts of Texas and Louisiana when the first white explorers arrived. Caddoan villages were usually flanked at the ends by platform mounds bearing temples or other important buildings. Caddoan pottery was unusually handsome, even for Mississippian work, which was nearly all superb. One archaeologist, A. D. Krieger, believes that the Caddoan area is the region through which fundamental Mississippian ideas entered the United States, moving out of Mexico into Texas and eastward to Louisiana. Others insist that Mississippian ideas spread westward from Louisiana into Texas and not the reverse.

The truth is uncertain at present. We cannot say whether the new ideas were carried out of Mexico through Texas to the Mississippi, as Krieger says, or if they arrived first in Mexican canoes landing on the shores of Louisiana, Mississippi, Alabama, or Florida. Nor is the spread of these ideas up the river fully understood; one school of thought holds that the ideas took root in the old Hopewell territory before traveling to other areas. There were probably several simultaneous thrusts, all getting under way about A.D. 700, with

Mississippian concepts spreading from centers on the lower Mississippi in Louisiana and farther to the north in the area between Memphis and St. Louis. Certainly by A.D. 900 most Indian tribes living along the Mississippi and its major tributaries knew something about the gospel of the platform-mound religion; within another three centuries, a chain of major ceremonial centers stretched from Oklahoma to Alabama.

2

Early commentators on the Mound Builders—even those who believed that all the mounds were the work of a single race—realized that there was something unusual about the giant flat-topped mounds found in the South and at a few points in the North. Squier noted that their distinctive form, "as well as their usually great dimensions, have induced many to regard them as the work not only of a different era, but of a different people." Relatively little work was devoted to these mounds in Squier's day, however, and he had no way of knowing that that guess was correct.

One of the first good accounts of the flat-topped mounds was that of William Bartram, who toured the Southeast mound region late in the eighteenth century. Among those he visited in 1773 were the Ocmulgee mounds, east of the present city of Macon, Georgia. This important group somehow went untouched by archaeologists throughout the nineteenth century. Finally in December 1933, the Smithsonian Institution's Bureau of American Ethnology began to excavate it. The program lasted eight years and involved the removal of tons of earth and the recovery of hundreds of thousands of artifacts. In 1938, A. R. Kelly, the first director of the Smithsonian's Ocmulgee work, published a report, which has been supplemented by more recent research.

Kelly uncovered a story with many chapters. About 3000 B.C. the Ocmulgee site was occupied by an Archaic people who left as evidence of their presence huge mounds of mussel, clam, and oyster shells, mixed with the bones of deer, bear, rabbit, turkey, and other wild creatures. About 2000 or 1500 B.C., these food-gathering folk learned how to make coarse pottery, thus taking a step toward Woodland Tradition life; about 1000 B.C. a farming settlement developed. Pumpkins, beans, sunflowers, and tobacco were the probable crops.

There seems to have been some contact between Ocmulgee and the Adena folk in early Burial Mound times. No burial mounds were constructed, but certain designs stamped on pottery have an Adena look, and there are other signs of a connection. Later—from A.D. 300 to 700—there was a large increase in population at Ocmulgee, and indications of Hopewell influence have been noted.

The first temple mounds at Ocmulgee date from about A.D. 900. They appear to have been the work of Mississippian folk who began an eastward migration from a point near St. Louis and in several generations reached central Georgia. These people cultivated corn as well as minor crops; they built a large village and established a major ceremonial complex. On the high ground above the river they constructed rectangular wooden temples and a circular chamber with a clay-covered wooden framework. Archaeologists believe that these were tribal community centers, the summer and winter temples where councils were held and rituals performed.

At the west end of the village rose a burial mound, which had been partly destroyed by railway construction when the 1933 excavations began. A careful vertical cut revealed that the mound consisted of a stack of five distinct flat-topped cones of clay. The innermost cone had six log-tomb burials beneath its base. A clay stairway of 14 steps had been built to reach the summit of this mound. Later, a second mound had been built above the first; it had had a building atop it, for the archaeologists found the outlines of poles in its clay summit. A third, fourth, and fifth flat-topped mound had been erected over this core, each time with a wooden building at the top. In the sod covering the last mound's summit were Indian burials of the late seventeenth century, containing such European artifacts as pipes and glass beads.

The Ocmulgee temple mound grew in the same way. Originally the temples had been at ground level, but they were frequently destroyed and rebuilt, and each time an old building was leveled a small platform was built as the foundation for the new one. Eventually one of these platforms was transformed into a great mound 50 feet high and some 300 feet at the base. Lesser temple mounds arose on top of it.

After two or three centuries, the Temple Mound people abandoned Ocmulgee. Perhaps the migrating urge that had taken them halfway across the continent came over them again about A.D. 1200; perhaps they were wiped out by the original people of the area; possibly there were religious reasons for moving elsewhere. The site was unoccupied in the entire Temple Mound II Period, from the thirteenth through the seventeenth centuries. Early in the eighteenth century Creek Indians, probably descendants of the Temple Mound folk, returned to the area to found a large and thriving community at the western edge of the site; the presence of knives, swords, bullets, flints, pistols, iron axes, and the like indicates contact with European traders, but these Creeks maintained their ancient festivals and at least some of their mound-top ceremonies for several generations. When William Bartram visited Ocmulgee in 1773, however, no Indians lived anywhere near the site.

Another spectacular Mississippian site is Etowah, near Cartersville in northern Georgia. Three great mounds rise here on the north bank of the Etowah River; the largest, a flat-topped pyramid more than 60 feet high covering over three acres, contains 4,300,000 cubic feet of earth. It is second in volume only to the Cahokia Mound among American earthworks.

De Soto may have visited Etowah. One account of his march mentions an Indian town called Guaxule that had an unusually large mound which "had round about it a road-way on which six men might march abreast." That description could refer to the big Etowah mound. But the first definite description of the Etowah group was the work of the Reverend Elias Cornelius, whose report was published in 1819. He called it "a stupendous pile," but said that the main mound "was so completely covered with weeds, bushes, and trees of most luxuriant growth that I could not examine it as well as I wished." He did manage to make fairly good measurements of the big mound. "On these great works of art," he wrote, "the Indians gazed with as much curiosity as any white man. I inquired of the oldest chief if the natives had any tradition respecting them, to which he answered in the negative. . . ." All that the Indians could say of the mounds was, "They were never put up by our people."

Several archaeologists visited Etowah between 1871 and 1873; by then the mound summits and surrounding plazas had been cleared of forest growth and were under cultivation. The Bureau of Ethnology began its explorations there in 1883, first under John Rogan, then under Cyrus Thomas. It was Rogan who brought to light the first of the famous Etowah copper plaques showing winged human figures wearing bizarre headdresses and eagle masks. Though their designs had the vivid, grotesque look of Aztec or Mayan art, Thomas shrewdly pointed out that they did not correspond to actual Mexican motifs; they had a Mexican flavor but were local artistic products. Later archaeologists would develop this idea into a major concept, the Southern Cult, a religious movement thought to have swept through the entire Temple Mound civilization about A.D. 1500.

W. H. Holmes of the Bureau of Ethnology excavated at Etowah in 1890; then the mounds were left undisturbed until Warren K. Moorehead investigated them in 1925. Moorehead was then a veteran of over 30 years of mound work—it was he who had excavated the original Hopewell Mound in 1891-92—and his Etowah dig was the crowning of a notable career. He spent parts of three winters there, excavating the village site and the third largest mound, a structure 22 feet high and 180 feet in diameter at its base. He took this mound apart completely, replacing the earth afterward. In it he found swords and knives of seemingly Mexican style; pottery vessels in color; discs of shell with engraved designs of woodpeckers, human figures in antlered head- es, and severed heads, together with other artifacts bear-

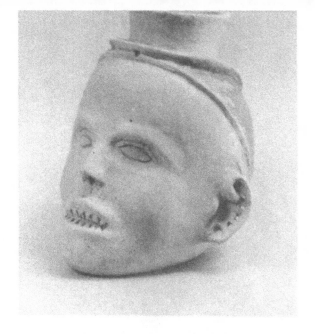

42   Effigy jar from Fortune Mound, Arkansas. Courtesy
Peabody Museum, Harvard University.

43   Effigy vessel from Pecan Point, Arkansas. Courtesy
Museum of the American Indian, Heye Foundation,
New York.

44   Kneeling man effigy from Temple Mound, Tennessee. Courtesy Frank H. McClung Museum, University of Tennessee, Knoxville, Tennessee.

ing equally strange and oddly awe-inspiring motifs. Moore-head believed that Etowah was the dominant village, "the hub," of a widespread culture whose hallmark was this mysterious style of art. He suggested that a Mexican group from eastern Yucatán had migrated through the West Indies into Florida and, after long occupation there, had moved northward into the southern United States and on up the Mississippi Valley, constructing huge earthen mounds as they went.

Artifacts in the Etowah style came to light at a number of other major Temple Mound sites. Perhaps the most intense expression of the style was found at the huge ceremonial center of Moundville, on the Black Warrior River in northern Alabama.

Moundville consists of nineteen square and oval flat-topped mounds, from 3 to 23 feet in height, arranged in a rough circle about two others, 22 and 57 feet high. The shorter of these covers the greatest area of any in the group, 195 by 351 feet. On the north side of the taller central mound is an artificial platform about 1⅔ acres in size. Most of the mounds have one or more graded ramps leading to their summits.

Clarence B. Moore, in 1905 and 1906, excavated 560 burials in and around the mounds. The artifacts in the grave included pottery, discs of shell and stone, and pipes, using such designs as the swastika, the human hand, skull, eye, and arm, the eagle, the woodpecker, the heron, and the horned toad. Winged snakes are occasionally shown, calling to mind the Feathered Serpent motif famous in Mexico. Some of the images are grotesque; one double-headed figure has a heron's neck, a woodpecker's fanlike tail, and a serpent's long tongue. The intricate symbolic designs from

Moundville evoke a mood of brooding fantasy. Here are profiled skulls with great toothy jaws; here are staring eyes without faces, some of them weeping; here are bodiless hands; here are crosses within circles; eyes sprouting in the palms of hands, fingers pointed to nowhere; terrifying beaked birds, men with frightening masks, and a host of weird geometrical forms. The flavor, as at Etowah, is Mexican; but the design motifs, eerie and haunting, are nearly all unique to the Temple Mound II Period of the United States.

This style of art was not confined to Alabama and Georgia. It has been found as far west as the Spiro Mound in eastern Oklahoma. There are at Spiro eight mounds of varying sizes; the largest one had been used both as a temple mound and as a burial site, and contained a rich collection of artifacts. A great tragedy of archaeology occurred here: a farmer plowing at the base of the mound accidentally exposed its contents, and he and his friends formed a company to "mine" the mound and sell the relics it held. They blew it open with dynamite and hauled out wheelbarrow loads of artifacts which they sold to dealers, collectors, and museum purchasers. Within two years the site was all but destroyed for scientific purposes.

Archaeologists finally took over at Spiro in 1935, and the following year the University of Oklahoma began a program of excavation that lasted until 1941. It had surprising success at salvaging artifacts and data from the vandalized mound group. Meanwhile, a dedicated pair of amateur archaeologists, Mr. and Mrs. H. W. Hamilton of Missouri, spent some 16 years tracing the scattered Spiro objects that had been sold, gathering enough information to permit reconstruction of the Spiro society. Spiro had its own set of

45 Effigy figure from Spiro Mound, Oklahoma. Courtesy
Museum of the American Indian, Heye Foundation,
New York.

46 Wooden antler mask from Spiro Mound, Oklahoma. Courtesy Museum of the American Indian, Heye Foundation, New York.

designs, but they are clearly akin to those found at Etowah and Moundville, and indicate definite cultural links between the Temple Mound people of Oklahoma and those of Georgia and Alabama.

3

This related assortment of symbols, design elements, and artifacts exerts a fascination as irresistible as that of the eerie Hopewell styles. Cyrus Thomas identified it late in the last century as something typical of the Southern mounds; Warren Moorehead, in 1932, speculated about a religious movement characterized by this strange style of art; a number of other archaeologists saw a kinship with the bizarre and grisly Mexican styles, particularly the style employed by the Toltec people of about a thousand years ago.

By 1941, these notions of a Southeastern religious movement influenced or even dominated by Mexico had crystallized into the theory of the Southern Cult—also known to archaeologists as the Southern Death Cult, the Buzzard Cult, and the Southeastern Ceremonial Complex. The theory was the work of A. J. Waring, Jr., and Preston Holder, whose pioneering paper analyzing the cult listed 51 identifying traits. Among them were:

Axes with head and handle made of a single piece of stone.

Stone batons or clubs.

47   Shell gorget from Spiro Mound, Oklahoma. Courtesy of the Museum of the American Indian, Heye Foundation, New York.

Shell pendants with background cut out to form crosses.

Copper pendants with circles or weeping-eye symbols.

Shell discs showing woodpeckers, fighting cocks, rattlesnakes, or spiders.

Pottery jars or bottles depicting circles, crosses, hands, skulls, rattlesnakes, flying horned serpents, and feathered serpents.

Copper plates showing warriors in eagle costumes, sometimes carrying a human trophy head in one hand and a baton in the other.

The idea of the Southern Cult, with its distinctive style of art and its chain of ceremonial centers stretching across the whole lower half of the nation, stirs the imagination in a way that mounds alone, however massive, cannot do. It brings the Temple Mound people to vivid life in the same way that the sight of the Newark octagon, for example, gives life to the Hopewells. We are free to conjure up impressive processions to the tops of the great mounds, strange rites within the temples at their summits, the blaze of a sacred fire atop the vast earthen heaps, perhaps ritual human sacrifice. There is a touch of fantasy about the Southern Cult art that excites our wonder. The mounds become the platforms for lost cathedrals. The poetry, the history, the names of the kings of the mound folk, are forever lost to us; but here are wands, scepters, holy plaques, ritual vessels, all evoking elaborate ceremonies shrouded by time, all decorated with the nightmarish figures that these people held sacred.

Archaeologists explain the cult movement in several ways. The first view of it, one that still appeals to many, is that it sprang up early in the sixteenth century in response to de Soto's bloody and disastrous march across the Southeast.

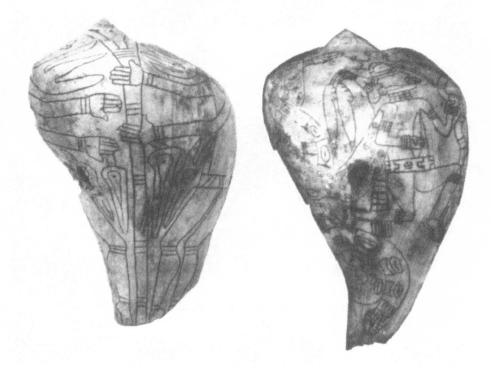

48   Incised conch shell from Spiro Mound, Oklahoma.
      Courtesy Museum of the American Indian, Heye
      Foundation, New York.

49   Incised conch shell from Temple Mound, Oklahoma.
      Courtesy Museum of the American Indian, Heye
      Foundation, New York.

The route of the Spaniards ran through almost the whole of
the cult-center area, and de Soto's policy of calculated mur-
der along the way undoubtedly sent a shock wave rippling
through the numerous farming settlements he visited. Other
students trace the cult to an earlier shock wave: that caused
by the Spanish conquest of Mexico in 1519. The toppling
of the mighty Aztec empire very likely echoed into the land

50 Temple Mound burials, Wycliffe, Kentucky. *Photograph by Barbara Silverberg.*

of the Temple Mound folk—particularly if there was frequent contact between Mexico and the United States at that time. The doom of the Aztecs might well have inspired the birth and swift growth of a somber cult among those to the north who guessed correctly that their turn to be conquered would come next.

These dramatic theories have been deflated somewhat by the hard truths of carbon-14 dating. It begins to look as though the cult—if it really was a cult—existed as early as the fourteenth century, maybe even earlier. A 1964 study yields for one of the Spiro mounds a series of dates from A.D. 818 to 1084. It now is thought that the Spiro center flourished between A.D. 800 and 1100 and died out by 1250. If this is so, the cult may have begun at Spiro, spreading northward and eastward to reach such centers as Moundville and Etowah in the fifteenth and sixteenth centuries.

In that case, the cult could not have been a movement expressing despair over the Spanish invasions. A. J. Waring, Jr., has suggested that the Temple Mound religion was an expression of vitality rather than of terror, and that the symbols we find so frightening were only emblems of harvest and renewal. But carbon-14 dates are still subject to revision, and it may yet be found that the cult was a sixteenth-century development, a reaction to the menace of the white-skinned strangers.

4

Many important Mississippian sites lie outside the Southeast. The greatest mound structure of all, Cahokia, is one such outlying earthwork. Cahokia Mound is the central feature of what may once have been a group of several hundred mounds in Madison County, Illinois. About eighty survive today, though some have been destroyed in recent years by highway construction; the heart of the group is preserved in the 225-acre Cahokia Mounds State Park, just east of the industrial city of East St. Louis, Illinois.

The giant main mound is so huge that it seems to be only a natural hill until one notices its flat-topped outline. It is about 1,037 feet long and 790 feet wide, rising to a maximum height of some 100 feet and covering 16 acres. Its volume has recently been calculated at 21,976,000 cubic feet, five times as great as that of the next largest mound, at Etowah. Cahokia rises in four terraces, now much obliterated by erosion and vegetation. Smaller, dome-shaped mounds cluster about it.

Cahokia's prehistory goes back well beyond the Temple

51 Cahokia Mound, Illinois. Courtesy Illinois State
Museum, Springfield, Illinois.

Mound Period, but little is known of the early phases. Evidently Woodland Tradition settlements gave way in Temple Mound I to a transitional Mississippian village, which blossomed in Temple Mound II into an immense political and religious center. Carbon-14 dating indicates that the great mound was built between the years A.D. 900 and 1250 in a series of extended stages; after centuries of work on it, the Cahokia people apparently stopped construction with the structure still incomplete, and began building the smaller mounds that surround it. It is thought that Cahokia was colonized by Mississippian folk coming up the river from the South, but this idea, like much else currently believed about Cahokia, may have to be discarded once the results of excavations begun there in 1964 have been fully analyzed.

One interesting suggestion, based on data discovered between 1960 and 1963, is that Cahokia may have served as a sort of solar observatory. Four precise circles, 240 to 480 feet in diameter, were once laid out with posts near the mounds; it is suggested that they were sighting points for calculating the position of the sun at the time of the changes of seasons. Perhaps the Cahokia farmers forecast the best planting times by observing the sun's relative position by means of these posts.

The colossal center at Cahokia was abandoned in the sixteenth or early seventeenth century. French explorers later in the seventeenth century passed close to it without seeing any sign of a settlement. From 1809 to 1813 the village was inhabited by French monks, from whom the great mound took its early name, Monks' Mound. Many nineteenth-century travelers visited the mound, and a number of amateur archaeologists dug in it for pots, but there was no scientific examination of the Cahokia site until 1922. It is now the scene of considerable archaeological activity.

There are other important Temple Mound II sites in the area, such as Angel (outside Evansville, Indiana, a few hundred miles east of Cahokia) and Kincaid (on the Ohio River opposite Paducah, Kentucky). These have both undergone thorough scientific exploration. River routes carried the Mississippian Tradition also into Tennessee and Arkansas, Missouri, and Kentucky. In Arkansas and Tennessee, particularly, high artistic levels were reached. The human-effigy pottery of Temple Mound II times was unusually fine, portraying the faces of strange-looking men with decorated cheeks and mouths, and slitted eyes that may represent dreaming or, more likely, death. That touch of the bizarre so typical of the Temple Mound people was never more strongly demonstrated than in these effigy pots of the Tennessee Valley.

5

The end came. We do not know how and why. It is simplest to say that the Temple Mound cultures were shattered by the arrival of the white man, with his contagious new diseases and his habit of enslaving the peoples he met. No doubt de Soto and his successors had much to do with the disruption of a way of life that had grown complex and magnificent over some eight centuries. Certainly there were still many thriving centers of Temple Mound life when

52 Effigy vessel from the Tennessee Valley. *Author's collection, photograph by Barbara Silverberg.*

de Soto came in 1540; just as certainly, these centers were virtually abandoned by the late seventeenth century. We can easily imagine a combination of disease and despair snuffing out the villagers of the Southeast.

But though the Mississippians withered at the white man's touch, they seem already to have been declining when the Spaniards came. We have no prehistoric census figures, but the Frenchmen who occupied Mississippi at the beginning of the eighteenth century learned from the Indians themselves that even in regions that Europeans had never visited, the population had been decreasing for a long time. Epidemics of fever and smallpox seem to have been the cause.

Whatever the reason, the glory ebbed. Just as Adena and Hopewell had vanished, leaving simpler non-mound-building farmers in their place, so did the Temple Mound folk of the Southeast slide into a less ambitious way of life. Huge mounds were no longer built. The old ways lingered on feebly; around the old mounds the familiar festivals and rituals continued, but hollowly, until their meaning was forgotten and the villagers no longer knew that it was their own great-great-grandfathers who had built the mounds.

When white men came to the Southeast, they found a loose confederation of tribes in Georgia and Alabama, numbering some 30,000 Indians in 50 good-sized towns. The leaders of this confederation called themselves the Muskhogee, but English traders, meeting a branch of this tribe near a creek, called them the Creek Indians, and the name stuck. Other tribes in the same general part of the country spoke related Muskhogean languages; these were the Chickasaw and Choctaw Indians. Like the Creeks, they lived around the old temple mounds, and sometimes built low mounds of their own on which to place temples and dwellings of chiefs. To the north of these Muskhogean-speaking peoples lived the Cherokees, whose language was Iroquoian, indicating they had come from the west and north. Except for language, the Cherokees were similar in culture to their Muskhogean neighbors.

All of these Indians of the Temple Mound region had only faint and foggy notions of their own history, and though it seems likely that the Creeks were direct descendants of the Temple Mound people, nothing in Creek myth confirms that idea. Only one group of Southeastern Indians still maintained a real link to its Temple Mound heritage when the white men arrived: the Natchez, a Muskhogean tribe living in seven small villages east of the present city of Natchez, Mississippi. We know a great deal about these people, largely due to the writings of French traders who lived among them from 1698 to 1732.

At the center of the Natchez villages was Emerald Mound, a 35-foot-high mound covering seven acres. But each village had its own temple mound and a mound for the chief's dwelling. The French writers described these mounds in detail; they also give us unique and valuable information on the social system of the tribe. If we are correct in thinking that the Natchez were the last representatives of Mississippian culture, this material is our only real clue to the nature of tribal life among the Temple Mound folk.

The Natchez government was an absolute monarchy. At its head was a ruler called the Great Sun, who was considered divine and had total power over his subjects. "When he [the Great Sun] gives the leavings of his dinner to his brothers or any of his relatives," wrote one of the French observers, "he pushes the dishes to them with his feet. . . . The submissiveness of the savages to their chief, who com-

mands them with the most despotic power, is extreme . . .
if he demands the life of any one of them he [the victim]
comes himself to present his head."

The Great Sun's foot never touched the bare earth. Wearing a regal crown of swan feathers, he was carried everywhere on a litter, and when he had to walk, mats were
spread before him. He and a few priests were the only ones
permitted to enter the temple atop the mound, where an
eternal fire burned and the bones of previous Great Suns
were kept. When a Great Sun died, his entire household—
wife and slaves—was killed to accompany him into the
afterlife.

The immediate relatives of the Great Sun were members
of an aristocracy, the "Suns." All the important officials of
the tribe were chosen from the Suns. Beneath the Suns in
importance was a class called the "Nobles." Beneath them
were the "Honored Men," and at the bottom was a large
class of despised and downtrodden commoners known as
"Stinkards." The class divisions were sharply drawn and
there was no way to rise; once a Stinkard, always a Stinkard.

The unusual feature of this class system is the way it
evolved from generation to generation. All Suns including
the Great Sun himself were required to marry Stinkards.
Thus every Sun was the child of a Sun and a Stinkard. The
children of female Suns were Suns themselves, but the children of male Suns were demoted to the Noble class. The
son of the Great Sun, therefore, could never succeed his
father, for he would be only a Noble. The Great Sun's successor was usually one of his sisters' sons, who, since Sun
rank descended through the female line, was himself a Sun.

Nobles also had to marry Stinkards. The children of
female Nobles were Nobles also; the children of male Nobles

were demoted one class and became Honored Men. It worked the same way among them: the children of male Honored Men became Stinkards. Since there were always a great many more Stinkards than members of the three upper classes, most Stinkards married other Stinkards, and their children, of course, were Stinkards too. But a good many Stinkards became mates for Suns, Nobles, or Honored Men, and so their children were able to rise to higher classes. It was an intricate and clever system, which guaranteed constant transfusions of new blood into each of the four classes. We do not know, of course, whether this unusual arrangement was found among all Temple Mound peoples. Possibly the Natchez, the last survivors, evolved this extremely complex social structure themselves as their culture's final surge of creativity.

The Natchez rebelled against the French in 1729. In a prolonged and bloody campaign they were all but wiped out; the survivors became scattered among other Southeastern tribes, who looked upon them as gifted with mystic powers.

The Creek Indians, who were still numerous when the white men came, appear to have been Temple Mound folk who had forgotten their ancestry, though they recalled the ancient customs to some extent. A typical Creek town was arranged around an open plaza, with the chief's house at one end and a ceremonial building at the other. These important structures were usually elevated on low mounds.

The center of the plaza contained two important features: the Hot House, or winter temple, and the open court where the game of *chungke* was played. The Hot House was a round building 50 feet in diameter, plastered with mud. Women never entered the Hot House. Each warrior of the tribe had his own bench in it; he would go there to smoke his pipe or rest or talk with his friends—a kind of men's club. An adjoining open cabin served the same purpose in summer.

Chungke, or "chunkey," was the popular game of the Southeast, and it seems to have been of great antiquity, going back to Adena–Hopewell times. It was played by two men using 8-foot poles tapered to flat points at their ends. One man would bowl a stone disc, 5 inches across and 1½ inches thick, down the field, and both players, running abreast, would hurl their poles like javelins toward the stone. The player whose stick landed closer to the point where the stone stopped rolling scored a point; if his pole actually touched the stone, he scored two points.

The Creeks were divided into two groups, the "Whites" and the "Reds," each including some twenty-five clans. They were also divided into Upper and Lower Towns. The White Clans were Peace Clans; the Red, War Clans. All the peacetime responsibilities of Creek life were supposed to be handled by the White Clans of the Upper Towns. The *miko,* or principal chief of the confederacy, was always chosen from a White Clan. White Towns were sanctuaries for fleeing murderers. The clansmen of the Upper Towns were charged with carrying out such civil ceremonies as the *puskita,* the eight-day-long summer-harvest festival. On the other hand, all the ceremonies of war were the affair of the Lower Towns; members of the Red Clans were supposed to organize war parties, lead raiding expeditions, and perform the religious rituals having to do with war.

The division between Upper Towns and Lower Towns soon became blurred; many of the Lower Towns were actually north of the Upper Towns as some tribes changed residences. And in most villages both Red and White Clans could be found, although the chief always came from a White Clan.

These customs were already breaking down when the white man shattered Creek culture in the eighteenth century. Creek lands were gradually nibbled away, and in 1830 Congress passed a law taking from the Indians all territory that they still held east of the Mississippi. The Creeks and their neighbors, the Choctaws, Cherokees, and Chickasaws, were removed at government expense and given land in Oklahoma. Though the tribes have survived there and have become prosperous, due in part to oil wealth, few traces of their ancient ways remain.

Outside the Temple Mound heartland, Indians who had no real part in the mound-building enterprise seem to have acquired the habit in a small way during the seventeenth century. Among them were the Cherokees. When European explorers entered Tennessee and the Carolinas in the seventeenth century, they found the Cherokees in command of a vast region along the Tennessee Valley. They were at constant war with their neighbors, particularly the Creek Indians to the south and the Chickasaws to the west. By most reports, the Cherokees had not been in the area long, but had come as invaders from another region.

Cyrus Thomas wrongly thought the Cherokees had built the great Ohio mounds before their migration to the Southeast. The Cherokees themselves, though, looked upon the mounds as the work of an earlier people. Some "mounds" did exist in the Cherokee villages; but archaeological work carried on in the 1930's showed that these were neither burial mounds nor temple mounds, but merely the ruins of a series of Cherokee community centers, each built atop the one before it until a good-sized mound accumulated on the site. By cutting trenches through the middle of these mounds, Cyrus Thomas failed to find the walls and other features of the buildings they contained, and so he did not realize that the Cherokee mounds were different from the other kinds of mounds built by earlier cultures.

We now know that the mound-building impulse faded gradually from the country. In Ohio, mound activity ended thirteen or fourteen centuries ago. In the Southeast, it lingered on into the late seventeenth or early eighteenth century. In the far North, the effigy-mound people were building their low pictorial mounds until the late eighteenth century. There is good evidence that occasional mound burials continued in the Great Plains well into the nineteenth century, but only the greatest chiefs were awarded this honor.

For a thousand years the Adenas had heaped up earth; for five centuries after their passing, the Hopewells had reared their impressive enclosures and embankments; and then, while Europe was passing through the upheavals of the Crusades and the Black Death and the Renaissance, the builders of temple mounds constructed their titanic platforms. After that came a swift and puzzling decline, and an end to the mound-building urge.

Grass and shrubbery sprouted on the slumbering mounds. Saplings grew to mighty trees. Those in whose veins ran the blood of Hopewells or Temple Mound folk slipped back toward savagery. Then came the white man, who stared, and wondered, and speculated, and spoke of vanished races. The mythmakers did their work, and the sober-minded archaeologists undid the myths, and the bulldozers came to destroy many of the mounds that had inspired the myths. And yet some mounds remain, famous in their own vicinities, although virtually unknown to Americans outside the mound

zone. It is difficult now to understand how intensely interested people were in the mounds and their builders a century
and more ago, and we have trouble realizing why people
were so eager to believe that the mounds were the creations
of superior beings hidden in the mists of time. The old
myths are dead, and archaeologists smile at the fancies of
yesteryear.

Yet there is magic in the mounds even now. Forget the
labors of Cyrus Thomas and the other debunkers; cast from
your mind the diligent toil of William Webb and Don Dragoo and Olaf Prufer and James Ford and Warren Moorehead and Henry Shetrone and William Mills and all the
other archaeologists who have shown us why we must not
think of the builders of the mounds as the Mound Builders.
Stand in the midst of the Newark octagon on a summer
afternoon, or walk along Fort Ancient's wall, or scramble to
the top of Cahokia, or look down from the observation
tower upon Great Serpent Mound. All is green and silent;
and, looking about at these mysterious grassy monuments,
one surrenders easily to fantasy, and feels the presence of the
ghosts of departed greatness, and then, in warm understanding, one reaches out across the decades to the makers of the
Mound Builder myth.

53 Outer wall of the South Fort, Fort Ancient. *Photograph by Barbara Silverberg.*

BIBLIOGRAPHY

▲▲▲

Atwater, Caleb. *Description of the Antiquities Discovered in the State of Ohio and Other Western States*. American Antiquarian Society, 1820.

Bakeless, John. *The Eyes of Discovery*. Dover Publications, New York, 1950.

Baldwin, J. D. *Ancient America in Notes on American Archaeology*. Harper & Brothers, New York, 1872.

Bartram, William. *The Travels of William Bartram*. Yale University Press, New Haven, 1958.

Billington, Ray Allen. *Westward Expansion: A History of the American Frontier*. The Macmillan Company, New York, 1949.

Boland, Charles Michael. *They All Discovered America*. Doubleday & Co., Garden City, New York, 1961.

Brandon, William. *The American Heritage Book of Indians*. American Heritage Publishing Co., New York, 1961.

Caldwell, Joseph R. and Robert L. Hall, editors. *Hopewellian Studies*. Illinois State Museum, Springfield, Ill., 1964.

Donnelly, Ignatius. *Atlantis: The Antediluvian World*. Gramercy Publishing Co., New York, 1949.

Dragoo, Don W. *Mounds for the Dead*. Carnegie Museum, Pittsburgh, 1963.

Ford, James A. "Mound Builders of the Mississippi." *Scientific American*, Vol. 186, No. 3, 1952.

Foster, J. W. *Prehistoric Races of the United States of America*. S. C. Griggs and Co., Chicago, 1874.

MacGowan, Kenneth and Joseph A. Hester, Jr. *Early Man in the New World*. Doubleday & Co., Garden City, New York, 1962.

Myron, Robert. *Shadow of the Hawk: Saga of the Mound Builders*. G. P. Putnam's Sons, New York, 1964.

Pidgeon, William. *Traditions of De-coo-dah*. Horace Thayer, New York, 1858.
Prufer, Olaf H. "The Hopewell Cult." *Scientific American*, Vol. 211, No. 6, 1964.
Putnam, Charles E. *A Vindication of the Authenticity of the Elephant Pipes and Inscribed Tablets*. Glass & Hoover, Davenport, Iowa, 1885.
Shetrone, Henry C. *The Mound Builders*. D. Appleton, New York, 1930.
Silverberg, Robert. *Home of the Red Man*. New York Graphic Society, Greenwich, Conn., 1963.
——— *Man Before Adam*. Macrae Smith, Philadelphia, 1964.
——— *Mound Builders of Ancient America: The Archaeology of a Myth*. New York Graphic Society, Greenwich, Conn., 1968.
——— *The Old Ones: Indians of the American Southwest*. New York Graphic Society, Greenwich, Conn., 1965.
Squier, E. G. and E. H. Davis. *Ancient Monuments of the Mississippi Valley*. Smithsonian Institution, Washington, D.C., 1848.
Thomas, Cyrus. *Report on the Mound Explorations of the Bureau of Ethnology*. Smithsonian Institution Bureau of Ethnology, Twelfth Annual Report. Washington, D.C., 1894.
Webb, William S. and Raymond S. Baby. *The Adena People, No. 2*. Ohio Historical Society, Columbus, 1957.
Webb, William S. and Charles E. Snow. *The Adena People*. University of Kentucky, Lexington, 1945.
Willey, Gordon R. *An Introduction to American Archaeology*, Vol. 1. Prentice-Hall, Englewood Cliffs, N.J., 1966.

INDEX

▲▲▲

Adair, James, 29
Adena Culture, 76, 171, 176, 177, 178–179, 180, 184–190, 194
  comparison of, with Hopewell Culture, 179–180, 218
  duration of, 181
  relation of, to Hopewell Culture, 199–201
  See also Cresap Mound
Adena Mound, 169, 189
Adena Pipe, 177
Alligewi, 46–48
Altar Mounds, 90
Amalgamation Mound, 104
American Anthropological Association, 170
American Antiquarian Society, 50, 98
American Ethnology Society, 64, 82, 83
American Indians, 9, 11, 23, 43
  Florida, 16–19, 21
  Hopewells identified as, 202
  mound-building, 24, 28
  Mound Builders relation to, 57, 112, 113, 139, 160, 168–169
  See also Gallatin
American Indians, History of the, 29
American Philosophical Society, *Transactions of the,* 40, 41
Angel, 257

Anthropological Association, American, 170
archaeology, 50, 61, 63
  salvage, 180, 181, 201
archaeologists, problems of, 170–171
art, Mound Builders', 94
Atlantis theory of Mound Builder survival, 144–149
Atwater, Caleb, 84, 151, 162, 164, 191, 204
  Circleville earthworks described by, 53–54, 55
  diffusionism upheld by, 57
  Haven's comment on, 98
  Hopewell Group visited by, 212, 213
  Ohio mounds study by, 50–56, 80, 82
  quoted on Grave Creek Mound, 75–76
  theories of, concerning Mound Builders, 45, 57–60, 87
Aztalan Mounds, 239
Aztec culture, mounds related to, 12

Baby, Raymond S.,
  Adena mound excavation by, 180
  death mask reconstructed by, 208
Baily, Francis, 41
Baldwin, John D., 113–116

270

Bancroft, H. H., 109
Barton, Benjamin Smith
  Haven's comment on, 98
  mound-building theories of, 32–33, 42
Bartram, John, 34
Bartram, William, 33–39, 84, 161
  mounds discovered by, 35–39
  Ocmulgee visited by, 240, 243
Behemoth: A Legend of the Mound-Builders, 67–68
Bing, M. Levy, 78
Blackmore, William, Mound Builder relics bought by, 97
Blumer, Reverend Ad, 122, 123
Book of Mormon, 70, 111
  possible source of, 72
Brackenridge, H. H., 56
British Museum (London), Mound Builder relics in, 97
Bryant, William Cullen, 66–67
Bullen, Ripley P., 226
burial mounds, 29, 36, 40, 188
  conical, 12, 171, 177
  Hopewell, 205–206
  Ohio's, 54, 90
  Wisconsin's, 154

Caddo Culture, 239
Cahokia Mound, 10, 27, 64, 88, 95, 165, 192, 235, 238, 243, 255, 256–257, 266
California, University of, 225
carbon-14 dating, 174, 180, 181, 187, 197, 222, 224, 226, 254, 255, 256
Cherokees, 37, 38, 47–48, 160–161, 163, 260, 264
Chickasaws, 37, 259, 264
Choctaws, 37, 259, 264
Cincinnati Tablet, 95
Circleville (Ohio), 50, 53–54, 105
Clinton, DeWitt, 46, 84
Cofachiqui, 21, 22–23
Colden, Cadwallader, 28

Coles Creek Culture, 238
Conant, A. J., Pidgeon diagrams used by, 109
Copena Culture, 201
Cornelius, Reverend Elias, 243
Cowan Mound (Ohio), 187
Crania Americana (Morton), 80, 81, 194
Creek Indians, 36–37, 243, 259–260, 263–264
Cresap Mound, 181–84, 187, 188, 220
Crookham, George, 125–126
Crystal River Complex, 224–225, 226
culture, definition of, 171
cultures, local series of, 173
Cutler, Rev. Manasseh, Marietta tree-ring dating by, 32

Darwin, Charles, 111
Davenport Academy of Natural Sciences
  "elephant pipes" acquired by, 122–123
  Henshaw's criticisms resented by, 136, 138–143
  Thomas's opinion of, 166
Davenport (Iowa) mounds
  artifacts found in, 121–123, 138, 166
Davenport Public Museum, 143
Davis, Dr. E. H., 85, 139, 142, 162, 164, 191, 207, 208
  criticism of, by Henshaw, 132–134
  Haven's comment on, 98
  Hopewell excavations by, 212–213
  Squier's associate, 82, 83, 91
Death Mask Mound, 208
De-coo-dah, 99, 102–109, 111
de Soto, Hernando, 16–24, 26, 84, 252–253, 258–259

diffusionism vs. independent invention, 57
Dixon, Roland B., 170
Donnelly, Ignatius T. T., 145–149
Dragoo, Don W.,
  comments by, on Adena Culture, 186–188, 198–199, 200
  work of, on Cresap Mound, 181–184, 220
Drake Mound (Kentucky), 181
Drucker, Philip, 225

Eagle Mound, 204
Edwin Harness Mound, 169
effigy mounds, 12, 13, 90, 233
  See also Wisconsin
effigy pipes, 189
"elephant mound," Wisconsin, 135, 136, 148
elephant pipes, 148
  of Davenport, Iowa, 121, 122
  Henshaw's comment on, 136
Emerald Mound, 260
Emmert, John W., 154
Ethnology, Bureau of American, 63, 64, 125, 129, 143, 153
  Annual Reports of, 15, 130, 131, 136, 137, 139, 154, 162
  Etowah explorations by, 244
  Ocmulgee excavations by, 240
  Putnam's criticism of, 138, 139, 141
Etowah Mound, 154, 156–58, 243–247, 248, 250, 255

Five Nations, History of the, 28
Florence Mound (Ohio), 187
Florida
  mounds in, 169
  Indians in, 16–19, 21
  Spaniards in, 16–21
Ford, James A., 196–197
Fort Ancient, Ohio, 85, 100, 104–105, 169, 227–230, 231–232, 266
Fort Hill, Ohio, 85, 230

fortifications, mounds as, 85, 87
fossil evidence, 173–174
Foster, J. W., 138–139
  book by, 116–119
Fothergill, Dr. John, 34
French colonists in Southeastern U.S., 24–26

Gallatin, Albert, 63–64, 82
Gass, Reverend Jacob
  artifacts found by, 121–122, 143
  criticism of, by Henshaw, 136, 138
  defense of, by Putnam, 140, 141–142
  Thomas's opinion of, 166
Gentleman of Elvas, 17, 21
Grave Creek Mound, 41, 75–76, 88, 115, 177, 185, 186, 190
Grave Creek Tablet, 76–78, 165–166
grave goods, 189–190, 218
Gravier, Jacques, 27
Great Circle Earthworks, 204, 205
Great Debate, the, 74–124
Great Serpent Mound, 190–194, 266
Greenman, Emerson F., 178
Griffin, James B., theory of, concerning Hopewells, 227

Hale, Sarah, J., 66
Hamilton, Mr. and Mrs. H. W., Spiro artifacts recovered by, 248
Harpe, Bénard de la, 27
Harris, Rev. Thaddeus M., 41–42, 84
Harrison, Charles, 122
Harrison, William Henry, 61–63
Haven, Samuel F., 98–99
Heckewelder, John, 46–48, 113, 156, 161
Heizer, Robert F., 225
Henry, Joseph, 83

Henshaw, Henry W.
  carvings from mounds studied by, 132–136
  Gass criticized by, 136, 138
  Powell criticized by, 142
  Putnam's criticism of, 139, 141, 142
  Squier and Davis criticized by, 132–134
  Wilson criticized by, 134–135
Hildreth, Dr. Samuel, 53, 54
  metal objects found in mounds by, 151
Hiwassee Island Culture, 238
Holmes, William Henry, 137
Hopewell, Captain M. C., 204
Hopewell Culture, 194, 202–232
  comparison of, with Adena, 179–180, 218
  duration of, 181, 222
  end of, 227, 233
  origin of, 226
  relation of, to Adena, 199–201
Hopewell Mound Group, 169
  excavations at, 210–212
  Moorehead finds in, 213, 216
  Shetrone excavations at, 216–218

Indian Tribes (Schoolcraft), 78
Indian language study, 129
"Intrusive Mound Culture," 231
Israel, Ten Lost Tribes of, 43–44, 45, 59, 111, 114

Jefferson, Thomas, 39–40, 48
Joliet, Louis, 26, 27
Jones, David, 29

Kelly, A. R., Ocmulgee director, 240–241
Kincaid, 257
Kingsborough, Lord, 44
Koch, Albert, 120, 141
Krieger, A. D., 239

Landa, Diego de, 44
La Petit, Mathurin, 27

Lapham, Increase A., 97, 109
La Venta excavations, 225–226
Layard, Austin Henry, 111
Le Moyne, Jacques, watercolors by, 24–25
Lenni-Lenape, 46–48
Lewis, T. H., Pidgeon's work discredited by, 110–111
lost-race theories, 11, 15, 16, 41, 42, 154, 164, 169

McCulloh, Dr. J. H., Jr. 48–49, 80
McGraw, Alva, Hopewell artifacts on property of, 221–222
McKusick, Marshall, 142–143
McMichael, Edward V., 223–225, 226
Madison, Right Reverend James, 41, 42, 63, 84
"Madoc," 66
Mallery, Garrick, authenticity of tablets attacked by, 137–138
Mare, Peter, 122–123
Marietta mounds, 31–32, 41, 52, 53, 54, 55, 151
Marksville Culture, 237–238
Marquette, Jacques, 26, 27
mastodons, 121
  co-existence of man and, 119–120, 123, 135, 140, 141, 208–210
Mathews, Cornelius, 67–68
metal, Mound Builders' use of, 93, 151
Mexico
  Adena Culture traits theoretically linked to, 195–196, 198
  influence of, on Hopewells, 223–225
  Mound Builders linked to, 60, 63, 64–65, 114, 115, 149, 167
Miamisburg Mound, 13, 115, 177
Mica Grave Mound, 208
Middleton, James D., 154

Mills, William C.
  Adena Mound artifacts evalu-
    ated by, 176–178
  Mound City excavations by,
    208–210
  mound reports by, 169
Mississippi Valley
  earthworks of, 113
  first Europeans in, 26
*Mississippi Valley, Ancient Mon-
    uments of the,* 83–84, 96
Moore, Clarence B., 169, 247
Moorehead, Warren K.
  mound excavations by, 169, 212,
    244, 247
  speculation by, on art style, 250
Mormon Church, Mound Builders
    linked to founding of, 68, 72
Morton, Samuel G., mound skulls
    analyzed by, 79–81, 116, 194
Mound Builder controversy, 41, 119
  See also Great Debate, the
Mound Builder myth, 15, 16, 28,
    29–49, 50–73, 143, 174, 265–
    266
Mound Builder relics, Squier's
    collection of, 97
Mound Builders
  disappearance of, 95
  geometrical talents of, 161
  novels dealing with, 67–68
  origin of, discussed by Baldwin,
    113–116
  poetry concerning, 66–67
  See also American Indians,
    Toltecs
  pottery of, 92–93, 119
Mound City (Ohio), 207–210
Moundville (Ala.), 235, 247–248,
    250, 254–255
mound zones, 11, 265–266
mounds
  discovery of, 9–28
  flat-topped, 240

Mormon beliefs concerning, 72–
    73
New York, visited by Squier, 97
Northern, 28, 29
Powell's interest in, 126–127
religious uses of, 87
Southeastern, 33
types of, 12
  See also Ohio mounds; Wisconsin
Mount Royal, Florida, 35–36
Muskhogee, 259, 260

Narona, Delf, 186
Natchez Indians, 27, 260–62
National Geographic Society, 225
National Museum (Washington,
    D.C.), mound artifacts in, 137
Neanderthal skull, 111, 117, 118
Newark, Ohio
  mounds at, 87, 88, 95, 105, 116,
    204, 205, 266
  tablet inscriptions originating in,
    138
New World, man's arrival in, 173,
    174
Nineveh, finding of, 111
Norris, P. W., mound work of, 154

Ocmulgee mounds, 240–242, 243
Ocmulgee National Monument, 35
Octagon State Memorial, 205
Ohio Archaeological and Historical
    Society, 194
Ohio mounds, 29–33, 40, 48, 50–
    56, 61–63, 187, 190–194, 264–
    265
  Squier and Davis reports on, 83–
    97, 161–162
  Thomas booklet on, 161–162
  Whittlesey paper on, 97
  See also Hopewells, Miamisburg
Ohio State Museum, Hopewell
    grave goods in, 218
Oklahoma, University of, Spiro
    excavation program of, 248
Oppert, Jules, 77–78

Origin of Species (Darwin), 111
Ortiz, Juan, 18

Paleo-Indians, 174–175
Palmer, Dr. Edward, 154
Peabody Museum, Harvard's, 149–150, 169, 194
Penn, William, 44
period, definition of, 171
Periods
  Archaic, 173
  Burial Mound, 173
  Paleo-Indian, 173–175
  subdivisions of, 173
  Temple Mound, 173, 255–256
Pidgeon, William, 99, 102–109
  Wisconsin mounds excavated by, 100–101
  work of, discredited, 110–111
  See also De-coo-dah
Pipes, Mound of the, 208
population, mound-building related to, 56, 59, 95
Poverty Point mounds, 196–198, 234
Powell, Major John Wesley, 15–16, 125–128, 129, 130–132
  Indian language study by, 128
Pratt, Orson, 72–73
Pratt, W. H., 122–123
Pratz, Le Page du, 27
Priest, Josiah, 65–66, 227
Prufer, Olaf H., 203, 220–222, 223, 230, 231
Pueblo culture, 176
Putnam, Charles E.
  defense of Davenport Academy of Natural Sciences by, 138–143
  Gass defended by, 140, 141–142
  Henshaw criticized by, 139, 141
Putnam, Frederic W., 169
  curator of Harvard's Peabody Museum, 149–150

ideas of, concerning Mound Builders, 150–152, 155
interest of, in Great Serpent Mound, 191–194
Putnam, Brigadier General Rufus, Marietta mound map by, 31

Rembert's Mounds, 38–39
Ritchie, William A., 186, 198
Rittenhouse, David, 32
Rogan, John P., mound work of, 154
Ross County (Ohio), mound in, 13

Sargent, Colonel Winthrop, 40
Schliemann, Heinrich, 112
Schoolcraft, Henry Rowe, 78–79, 82
  Grave Creek Tablet examined by, 77
Schwab, Maurice, 77
Seip Mound, 169, 210–211
Shetrone, Henry C., 206, 208–210, 212, 216–218
Smith, Joseph, founder of Mormon Church, 68–73
Smithson, James, 83
Smithsonian Contributions to Knowledge, 83, 84, 97, 98
Smithsonian Institution, 97, 109, 124, 125, 139, 142, 143, 153, 174
  American Indian study by, 130
  involvement of, with Mound Builders, 83–84
  See also Ethnology, Bureau of American
Snow, Charles E., 178–179, 180, 190, 195, 200
Southern Cult, identifying traits of, 251–252
Southey, Robert, 66
Spaniards
  in Cofachiqui, 21–23
  in Florida, 16–21
Spiro Mound, 248, 254

Squier, Ephraim George, 97, 139, 142, 162, 164, 191, 204, 207, 208
  book by, on Ohio mounds, 83–97
  criticism of, by Henshaw, 132–134
  Haven's comment on, 98
  Hopewell excavation by, 212–213
  New York mounds visited by, 97, 156
  Ohio mounds explored by, 82–83
  quoted on flat-topped mounds, 240
Stiles, Ezra, 30–31
stone implements and ornaments, Mound Builders', 93–94

tablets, 94, 121–122, 138
Tallegewi, 46, 47, 156, 161
Taylor, Richard C., 90
Temple Mound People, 26, 233–267
temple mounds, 12, 13, 14, 26, 241
Tennessee Valley Authority, archaeological sites near, 178
teocallis, 12, 13
Thing, L. H., mound work of, 154
Thomas, Cyrus, 164–167, 168–169, 250, 264
  mound investigations by, 131, 137, 152–167, 265
  slayer of the Mound Builder myth, 131
Thompson, Daniel Pierce, 68
Toepfner Mound, 180
Toltecs, Mound Builders linked with, 33, 42, 115–116

Tomlinson, Abelard B., 76
tradition, definition of, 171
Traditions
  Archaic, 173, 175, 176, 237, 241
  Big-Game Hunting, 173, 175
  Mississippian, 173, 234, 235, 238, 239, 241, 257
  subdivisions of, 173
  Woodland, 171, 172, 173, 176, 234, 237, 238, 241, 256
tree-ring dating, 32, 85, 113
Troyville Culture, 238

United States Geological Survey, Powell as Director of, 128, 129
Ussher, James, world's age calculated by, 59, 111

Vega, Garcilaso de la, 19

Webb, C. H., 196–197
Webb, William S., 178–179, 180, 190, 195, 200, 201
Whittlesey, Charles, 97
Willey, Gordon R., archaeological work of, 170–171, 172, 173, 234
Wilson, Sir Daniel, criticism of, by Henshaw, 134–135
Wisconsin mounds, 97, 99, 104, 109, 135, 136, 148, 159
  Pidgeon's excavation of, 101–102
Woodland period, Late, 231
Works Progress Administration, archaeological program of, 178
Worthington, Thomas, Adena estate of, 176
Wyrick, David, 138

Zeisberger, David, 29